RAIN ON THE DESERT

RAIN ON THE DESERT

By

Gordon H. Fraser

MOODY PRESS
CHICAGO

ISBN: 0-8024-7153-6

Library of Congress Catalog Card Number: 75-15995

Printed in the United States of America

CONTENTS

1

RAIN ON THE DESERT

The hard, dry soil of the desert seems utterly unresponsive. The cacti are dull gray-green, the few clumps of creosote bush look as if they had given up the ghost, and the thorny ocotillo look like clumps of devil's whips.

Then the rain comes. Suddenly, as if from nowhere, the turquoise sky is a mass of thunderclouds. The rain cascades down in a deluge. The washes come alive with a torrent of red, muddy runoff.

A miracle occurs. The pungent scent of sagebrush and juniper becomes noticeable. The water seeps into the hard ground and awakens a million tiny seeds. In a few hours, a veritable carpet of tiny plants begins to appear; and, in another few days, the dry desert is a mass of colorful bloom. Botanists will be seen on their hands and knees with magnifying glasses, studying the small blooms that are not quite visible to the naked eye.

The ocotillo has put forth a mass of small, oval leaves which, in a few more days will fade and drop. Clusters of scarlet blossoms appear at the tip of each thorny stem. Even the cacti seem greener, and the saguaro will put forth a crown of creamy white bloom.

The tiny flowers mature and drop their seeds in a matter of days, and again the desert fades back into grays and browns.

But the miracle of regeneration has occurred. A life cycle has taken place, and the tiny new seeds drop to the ground to sprout and grow when the rain comes again, in months or even years.

Naturalists tell us that only half of the seed crop sprouts with each rainfall. The other half remains in the soil to sprout later, in case anything happens to the first crop of seedlings.

The pagan heart seems as hard as the desert soil; but, when the water of life penetrates, the seed is there and will respond. New seed is matured and sown to perpetuate the crop.

These are the stories of native American pagans, who, when the water of life sank down into their lives, came to life and matured as new creatures and then went out and reproduced.

2

NAVAJO

Navajo women have beautiful hands. While carding, spinning, and weaving the sheep's wool for their rugs, their skin is constantly being salved by lanolin, nature's own balm. The resulting softness of their hands would be the envy of their city-bred sisters.

The looms used by the Navajo women to weave their rugs have no shuttles. Every thread of the intricate patterns is placed by the deft fingers of the weaver, and every pattern—no two are alike—is drawn from the imaginative mind as it is being created.

Many Navajo men are silversmiths. Their silver and turquoise pieces are executed by hand tools. Molds for casting the solid silver are carved in sandstone. The flat work is hammered on anvils made from short pieces of railroad rail, which are salvaged as the men work laying tracks for the railroads.

When the Navajo couple goes to the trading post, she has her newly woven rug to trade for fabrics or groceries, and he has his pieces of jewelry to barter or sell.

The Navajos live in a vast area of desert, woodland, canyon, and mountain. The reservation, an area somewhat larger than the state of West Virginia, ranges in altitude from forty-two hundred feet, where the Little Colorado enters the Grand Canyon, to ten thousand feet, the summit of Navajo Mountain. Saltbush and ephedra at the lower levels give way to junipers and piñon at from fifty-five hundred to sixty-five hundred feet. Above this level, oaks give way to forests of ponderosa pine. At higher levels are forests of aspen and mixed conifers.

This tidy little subnation of 150,000 native Americans has lived happily for hundreds of years where a white society could not survive more than a few weeks.

About the time Columbus was battling the Atlantic gales with his tiny, unseaworthy caravels, the nomad Navajos were filtering southward into Arizona and New Mexico. The Déné tribes (they do not call themselves Navajos or Athapaskans) range all the way from the Mexican line to the Bering Strait, with a cluster of tribes on the Pacific coast north and south of the California-Oregon line. Other Déné tribes occupied areas along the Lower Columbia River until less than a hundred years ago.

Don't pity these dry-land dwellers as you pass through their reservation. Those refineries are processing Navajo oil, and those huge thermal-electric plants are fired by Navajo coal. Those are tribe-owned lumber mills, and all of the proceeds are deposited in the Navajo National Bank, with over one hundred million dollars in resources.

Poverty? Unemployment? White oriented sociologists came out with surveys that show 50 percent unemployment in the Navajo Reservation. Actually any Navajo can get a job with the tribe or a tribe-related industry. He is not unemployed; he is just not doing white-man jobs. He may choose just to stay home and herd the family sheep or make silver jewelry.

Underprivileged? No TV antenna? A survey made in Flagstaff, Arizona, showed less than 10 percent of the local TV programming to be of any interest to a Navajo.

Old age problems do not exist. Grandmother and grandfather are the elite of the family clan and have the best hogan. Family life is sacred to the Navajos. They always gravitate to the home clan area, and the focal point in each nuclear family is grandmother's hogan. The Navajos are matrilineal in their kinship pattern; and grandmother, her daughters, and their children constitute the family. Grandfather and the men who marry grandmother's daughters are from other clans and have their prestige in their own grandmothers' clans. The maternal uncles train and discipline their sisters' children. Grandmother and her daughters train the girls in the family clan. There are no orphans in the normal Navajo clan. Grandmother's daughters live nearby, and all of their children are considered siblings. If a natural mother dies, there is always an auntie to take care of the baby.

The Navajos *have* been underprivileged in spiritual matters. Missionaries were always handicapped by the vast area to be covered and by the fact that the language barrier has never even been dented. With the translation of the New Testament in 1956 and the resulting Navajo literacy, the Gospel is penetrating the barrier. Now, newly trained Bible institute graduates are going back to their people; and, for the first time in history, the indigenous church is emerging in the reservation.

3

DAVID BEGAY

The Navajos are artists, philosophers, and poets.

David Begay and I were standing on a rimrock overlooking the Jeddito Wash. A trickle of water was draining off the last of a summer downpour. Sheep were drinking at the potholes that were now filled with water.

To the southwest, the San Francisco peaks, the Navajo sacred mountains, were outlined against a blue sky. To the north were the Hopi mesas encrusted with the villages of the Peaceful People. The outlines of the ancient houses were visible if you knew where to look.

Below us a few cottonwood trees limned with green the gray banks of the wash. A few wisps of cloud lingered on the horizon. The sky-dome was turquoise.

Hogans and sheep corrals of the Naakaidineh clan dotted the gray-green sandscape.

There was no conversation; none was necessary. Each of us saw his own sort of beauty. To the white man, it was a strange waste of half-desert, with its own sort of almost sinister beauty, very vast and very silent. To the son of the clan, it was the home country.

Finally David spoke. One word was repeated three times at a few minutes' interval: *"nizhoni"* (it is beautiful). Each time there was an expressive sweep of the hand: first, toward the turquoise sky and the lone eagle that soared effortlessly; then, toward the enfolding hillsides and the gray-blue mountains beyond; last, toward the valley below—the little bands of sheep, the hogans of the clan, and the rimrock on which we stood. Each sweep of the hand with the softly spoken *"nizhoni!"*

David had spoken and demonstrated the very essence of the "Beauty Way Chant."

> Beauty above me,
> Beauty around me,
> Beauty beneath my feet.

David was a casualty of World War II. His disability made it unlikely that he would be able to work with the sheep on the reservation. He must seek employment of some sort. He hoped that it would not be in the white man's world.

In the war, he was one of those celebrated Indian intelligence operators with the built-in unbreakable code—the Navajo language. They could talk freely back and forth while the frustrated Japanese were trying to break this mystifying code. The Navajo boys could freely impart top-secret messages between units and even chat back and forth about what might be going on back home in Navajo land.

It was still more frustrating to the enemy when the Pima Indian men did the same thing but with a totally different but equally incomprehensible language. No one knows how much the skill of these Indian boys shortened the war.

David and a few members of his clan found the Lord Jesus some time after the war ended, and the simple, yet profound experience of salvation brought into adjustment many of the problems of the mind and life that had resulted from the war experience.

David committed his life to the Lord after one disconcerting experience in an utterly liberal mission that belittled the sacred Scriptures. David chose to believe his *God Bizaad* (lit., God, His Word—title of the Navajo New Testament). He was not only committed to the Lord but to his tribe and his own family clan. He must find some way to help his people and earn a living at the same time.

One function, available to alert Navajos, is that of interpreter. In the halfway life of the Navajo-English society, good interpreters are in demand. David would learn the skill. An interpreter must know the two languages well enough to think in both languages and be able to switch back and forth on a moment's notice. The war experience had been valuable training in this art, because many lives had depended on a correct and immediate interpretation of army tactics.

The new Navajo-language New Testament had become available soon after David left the service. He must learn more about it. He must have more schooling, and his schooling must relate not only to his job but, at the same time, enable him to be a witness to his own people.

Soon, David was sitting in class, his pencil poised and his Bible and notebook handy.

He was a thoughtful student. He responded only when spoken to but always with well-thought-out answers, which were always slightly delayed. He explained this later: he was practicing interpreting as he went along. He would hear the question in English, then translate it in his own mind into Navajo, then translate it back into English. He was an A student.

Before David was through school, a job opportunity was offered. He would be the interpreter for the relief office in his own county, which had a much greater Navajo than Anglo population. He would serve as interpreter to the caseworker in the county seat of St. John, Arizona.

We shuddered a little at this, because all of the white workers in his office were Mormons. But David had his feet on the Rock and was well prepared for any attempts at proselyting by his associates.

His work was so satisfactory that, within a matter of weeks, he was promoted to caseworker. He was doing most of the work anyway. Now he was conducting his work entirely with Navajos and in the Navajo language.

David came in to the school periodically and secured quantities of tracts and booklets in the Navajo language. He acquired visual aids to help teach his Navajo clients to read their own language and then secured Navajo New Testaments for their use.

On one occasion, he came in seeking a tape recorder. Clients, waiting their turn, could listen to the gospel in the Navajo language. He prepared a number of taped messages and kept them running while he worked. His English-speaking co-workers in the office never did learn what the tapes were saying; and, because his work was so efficient, they made no objections.

David's ministry extended far into the reservation, as his relief activities took him out into the hogans in one of the nation's largest counties. He witnessed as he traveled.

The county authorities admitted that they had never had such an efficient caseworker. He was being a missionary and getting good pay at the same time.

On weekends, David would leave for his home community on the banks of Jeddito Wash. Some months later—it was spring again—David visited the school.

"Will you come and speak at our camp meeting?" I asked.

"You have a camp meeting going?"

"Oh yes, and a church and Sunday school. All the Naakaidineh clan comes."

David and his uncle, Harry, had been busy. They had scrounged enough odds and ends of material to build a hogan chapel for the clan. Grandma Ruby's hogan was no longer big enough.

I arrived early, in time to see the clan assembling—teams and wagons, pickups, men and women on horses, some on foot. It was something like "the tribes coming up to Jerusalem." We would hear snatches of song, like the psalms of ascent in Solomon's time: "I was glad when they said unto me, let us go unto the house of the LORD."

Camp meetings are delightful occasions. No printed

programs. Much singing with the meadowlark charm of outdoor native-language singing. There were prayers and testimonies. There were confessions and pledges of forgiveness. There were messages by David and Harry, and a message from Hastiin from the Bible school, translated by David. There were no clocks to worry about. Today the sheep were all in the corral, and the sheepherders were present at the camp meeting. All took part as the Spirit moved them. There were smiles of delight and tears of repentance.

All the while, we could smell the tantalizing aroma of roasting mutton and the sizzling of "fry-bread." Coffee was bubbling in the big kettle. Just another Navajo feast? Well, yes and no.

A pause came, and one of the aunties announced that everything was ready. We gathered around, tin plates and cups in hand.

Our taste buds were reacting, and we hoped for a short grace, but Harry went on and on in prayer. All else was silence, except for the bleating of lambs and an occasional birdcall from the sagebrush.

It was all in Navajo, but I knew enough words to follow the thread of the prayer message. There was thanksgiving for the great work of redemption, something about the Lamb of God that took away the sin of the world. There was mention of the bread of life that came down from heaven. There was mention of the Passover feast at Jerusalem on the night that Jesus was betrayed. Then it dawned on me that this was the Lord's Supper being celebrated Indian style. We ate all of it in silence; and then, with delightful spontaneity, Grandma Ruby started to sing, and all joined in “My Jesus, I Love Thee!”

It was late in the afternoon, and the sun was on its way down the sky. There were some two hundred miles to go, and it would be dark before we reached home, but somehow the two hundred miles were lost in meditation.

This was the indigenous church in action, Navajo style.

4

JOHN TALLMAN

John came into the dean's office with a strange request. "I have to go over to Gallup and get my grandmother out of jail."

The dean hadn't heard that excuse before, but, strangely enough, it was a valid one. John's whole famly had a sad record of drunkenness and disturbing the peace. Their fondness for wild times in Gallup usually landed them in jail.

John's grandfather, two uncles, and a brother were medicine men. His grandmother was a shaman—a "handshaker." In the Navajo healing ceremonies, the handshaker diagnoses the ailment or the presence of an evil spirit by shaking a hand over the patient. The proper vibrations indicate the nature and location of the trouble. The other branches of Navajo medicine have a degree of legitimacy; the herb doctor follows a definite pattern of useful herbs, quite similar to the Chinese pharmacopoeia. The drummer and chanter and the sand painter produce a degree of psychological effect. The handshaker, by contrast, is a shaman or witch doctor.

John had been raised in such surroundings of sordidness, accompanied by the superstitious fear of the evil spirits. There is reason to assume that a degree of demon possession may exist in a number of the Navajo rites.

The Tallmans had always wanted John to become a medicine man. This involves rigid training by a medicine-man uncle, from about age seven to maturity. The candidate is urged not to go to the white man's school and to stay away from outside influence. He must spend endless hours studying the chants and the manipulation of the paraphernalia of the shamanistic art.

John escaped the training by various evasions, but he never got to school. He came to manhood with no knowledge of English and without being able to read his own language. He learned to drink at an early age and was quite dissolute by the time he was grown. He married a girl that he probably had met at a squaw dance.

There were Christian influences in the clan area, and a cousin, newly returned from Bible school, led John and his Desbah to the Lord.

John did not understand much about the process of salvation, but he did sense that it was a good clean escape from a previously sordid existence. John and his wife were persuaded to attend Bible school.

The family vehemently opposed the idea and finally threatened them with death if they went to the white man's school. Undoubtedly they tried to cause death by putting hexes on the young couple.

School is almost frightening to native people, away

from their clan area, facing teachers without being able to read in either language. This is a common problem in Navajo country. Probably 90 percent of Navajos still use only their own language in daily communication.

The school has a department where no English is used. All students speak Navajo, and the teachers are Navajos. The first problem to overcome is learning to read the native language. Sounds are matched with symbols, and after a few days it all begins to make sense. Within a few weeks, the Navajo student can read his New Testament quite freely. The doctrinal teaching always accompanies the learning process.

John was a good workman and paid his way handsomely in physical labor. Mrs. Tallman helped in the kitchen and in the print shop.

John felt constant pressure from the folks back in New Mexico. They would call him home on any pretext and then try to prevent his return to school. On one of his errands back home, he was coerced into taking a drink. He fell miserably and wandered around in the old way of life for several months, without motive or direction.

Desbah stayed at school and held on to the Lord in prayer for John. We all prayed, and God answered. Finally, John got sick of the devil's hog trough, and, with a desperate burst of determination, he showed up one evening at school, very crestfallen, wondering if we would have anything to do with him.

After a while on our knees together, talking to the Lord about it all, John agreed with us that, until he was stronger in the Lord, it would be fatal for him to visit his folks. He was discovering the hard truth of Luke 14:26: "If any man come to me, and hate not his father, and mother, . . . yea, and his own life also, he cannot be my disciple." John loved his folks but hated their way of life; someday he would make them disciples too.

John advanced well after his second start. It was not required of him that he study English: all of his work was in Navajo; but he decided to study English anyway, and he made good progress, studying the practical way, by always trying to speak with his fellow students in English when he was about his work. He was not afraid to try, and he would laugh at himself and his blunders when others laughed at his efforts. By the time his school years were over he was reasonably conversant in English. He was an excellent Bible student. The utter contrast between Bible study and the endless drilling of the old chants of the medicine men made him an appreciative student.

As he absorbed the teachings of the Word of God and the relationship with the Lord Jesus deepened, the scars of the old life faded away, and the "new man" was showing through. Desbah's spiritual life was enriched as she continued to intercede in John's behalf. She too matured into a real woman of God as she studied along with John.

There are personal work assignments that only a native can perform. In Flagstaff, many problems develop as the Navajo culture clashes with the white man's world. Flagstaff is such a large place to these desert dwellers that they call it Kinthlani, the Place-of-Many-Houses. They come in to town only in desperation.

They do most of their buying at the local trading posts on the reservation.

A family from Teasto had received word from Washington that their Ashkee would not be coming home from the war. They could not understand how or why the army could snatch their boy away from them and never send him back.

They acted as Navajo families do. The whole family loaded themselves into their pickups and traveled to Flagstaff, which was as near as they knew how to get to Viet Nam. Twenty-one of them came, from grandma and grandpa on down to the latest cradle-board baby.

They knew no English and could only show their letter from the government about their boy. Someone directed them to the rescue mission. They walked in as a body and were staying right there until someone could answer their question. Did we have someone at the school who could help?

John, made mature and tender by his recent experience, seemed to be the logical answer. We went downtown together, praying as we went, that we might be able to give some comfort and point them to the Saviour. I sat as obscurely as possible in a dark corner of the room while John greeted them in the soft Navajo speech. John soon sensed that they were not Christians and were very resentful.

Quiet conversation ensued. All of the adults in the group made little speeches about Ashkee. They wept silently; Navajos do not make demonstrations. John said little, just the *"ao"* of assent, until they were all through with what they had to say. Then he started to talk quietly with his Navajo Testament in his hand.

He read many portions, including the whole plan of salvation. There were many more questions and answers and much silent weeping when they realized that they would not see their boy again.

After two hours, they said their thanks as John committed them to the Lord. They filed out to their pickups and took their sad journey home.

It did not occur to us at the time that John had conducted his first memorial service. And it was a success because he had learned to weep with those who weep.

John and Desbah are back in their own clan area in New Mexico, pastoring a native church not many miles from where his grandparents are still beating their medicine drums and chanting. He hopes that they will see how much better his life is than theirs and will want to know this strange power that can make a clean man out of a miserable one.

5

HARRY RUSSELL

It was pouring rain as it can rain only in the high mountainous area around Flagstaff, Arizona. It was early, but such an evening as would tend to drive all sensible people into their homes and to their firesides.

The dean of the new Southwestern School of Missions was hoping for Indian students to make the school a reality. Any sort of students—daytime or evening! It would be unlikely, however, that anyone would come on this stormy night.

A pair of headlights blurred by the rain, a splashing of wheels in mudholes, and a banging of the door of a pickup truck announced the arrival of a visitor. A slender, youthful, and somewhat drenched Navajo knocked at the door.

"You Fraser?"

"Yes, that's my name."

"You teach English?"

"Yes, I teach English."

"You teach me? My name Harry Russell."

"Yes, I will be glad to teach you. When do you want to start?"

"How about right now? I here."

So, our language school had a start. Harry was a new believer and was now regretting that he had not spent more time in school when he had a chance. He had finished third grade.

Harry had a new Bible with good clear type, but he knew only the small common words. He worked hard for the Santa Fe Railroad, loading gondola cars at the cinder pit east of Flagstaff, and he lived in a railroad section house. Eight hours of hard labor followed by three hours of language study would be quite a heavy load, but Harry was determined that he was going to be a missionary to his people as well as a loader of freight cars.

Harry also had a wife, a former widow with several children, and now they had one of their own. We discovered that Harry had left them sitting in the pickup while he studied in a nice warm room inside. We quickly remedied that situation and brought the shivering wife and babes into the building and put them in the care of Mrs. Fraser, who knew no Navajo words at that time. Mrs. Russell knew no English. The three hours of noncommunication was somewhat broken by the old piano and a Navajo hymnbook. They could at least sing in their respective languages, and "Jesus Loves Me" has the same meaning in both languages.

We have often thanked the Lord for the Navajo hymnbook, a splendid one compiled by members of several Christian denominations, with white missionaries and native poets contributing to the contents. It is inspiring and gratifying just to run through the list of authors and translators. Missionaries of the Presbyterian, Christian Reformed, Methodist, Plymouth Brethren, and Independent churches share honors with Navajo men and women who, a few years before, were pagans. Now, a united company, they bring their praises before the throne. The Navajo Christians chuckle a little when they realize it is their hymnbook that has brought all of these competing missionary groups together in at least one regard.

So, the mixed sounds of English and Navajo singing being strained through the partition, Harry and I started to study. The simplest textbook for use in teaching English as a second language is the English Bible, and the Gospel of Mark is a good starting place; it is all narrative, and, since the gospels were written in a culture that knew sheepherding and farming in a semiarid country, the stories have real meaning.

We covered eight verses of the first chapter of Mark in three hours. New words had to be explained, grammatical constructions—so different from Navajo form—were studied, and the strange phonology of English had to be mastered sound by sound. Doctrines were encountered. Geography had to be studied which is strange to Navajos who think of the Navajo Reservation as being the world; they know in a vague way that there must be land and people out there, because the Santa Fe tracks bring trains out of the mountains to the east and send them over the mountain to the west.

Harry started to take notes for his own preaching. He had a fertile mind and was continually bringing in peripheral matter, which slowed the teaching process but always enriched it, bringing illustrations to Harry as well as the teacher. Stories had to be told. Harry would stop and say, "Want I tell story?" I would always say, "Yes, tell story." I did not want to miss any bit of lore.

Finally one night, we came in our study to the story of the Gadarene demoniac, and Harry was struggling with the pronunciation of the caption as it appeared in his Bible. A Navajo just could not get his tongue around such a set of English sounds, and Harry floundered. I said, "Don't worry about that, Harry, it is just the title of a paragraph. This man in the story was a man full of demons." As we studied the story, Harry grasped the significance of the situation and said, "That fellow just like me! Want I tell story?"

Study was suspended while Harry related the story of his own life as a pagan. It was a recounting of what is quite typical of an Indian's experience when he encounters the white man's culture with its liquor, gambling, fighting, and bad women, followed by the white man's jail and the accumulation of debts.

Harry continued, "My mudder, she say, Harry, your head full of bad spirits. I get medicine man to come and drive them away." A "sing" was arranged with its ceremony of several days' duration.

The Navajos have specialized medicine, like the whites. The fist practitioner is the "handshaker." He is the diagnostician. He shakes his hand over the patient to discover just where the evil spirit is located. Vibrations seem to tell him; this is pure shamanism. He prescribes the treatment.

The second practitioner is the artist who makes the

sand painting on the floor of the hogan where the treatment is to be given. This is a fascinating skill. Colored sand and clays are pulverized with a *mano* and *metate,* and the artist then produces a symbolic, and often quite intricate, design with the powdered sand. This may take an entire day to produce. The rite of sand painting was not native to the Navajos, who were nomads from the north country, but they adopted and perfected it when they came to the arid south where sand painting was practiced rather indifferently by the Yuman tribes living in the desert at the delta of the Colorado River. Much of the symbolism was borrowed from the ceremonially minded Hopi, who were in their present area long before the Navajo came south.

The sand painting serves as an altar, in the center of which the patient sits, stripped to the waist. The sand painting is supposed to draw off the ailment or the demons that are bothering the patient.

The third practitioner is the pharmacologist of the team. He is adept at using the native medicinal herbs. A potion is prepared, combining valuable ingredients as well as many items that have a significance to the doctor and are designed principally to make the potion bitter, hence valuable. The potion is administered to the patient by the hands of the medicine man while the patient sits quietly on the sand painting. As soon as the sand painting has served its purpose, it is immediately destroyed and the colored sand gathered up and scattered to the winds.

The final stage of the ceremony is the chanting. This practitioner is the psychiatrist of the team. He is a master of several chants that are most involved and have been memorized under the tutelage of a maternal uncle. The young disciple begins his training by the time he is eight years old and will continue until he is a mature man before he is permitted to practice his art. The chants may last from three to nine days. The chanter must perform the ceremony with meticulous detail and, if a mistake is made, must start the chant all over from the beginning. This would be quite shattering to the patient if the medicine man should make a mistake on the eighth day!

Harry's mother paid all of the practitioners their fees in sheep. The chanter then placed a silk band around Harry's head and instructed him to remain where he was for four days. Harry commented, "They chanted and drummed and called on all of the nature gods, but they didn't call on the right name. Two days later I was as drunk as ever."

A few weeks later Harry had touched bottom again, and two men, who later became students at Southwestern, found him lying in the ditch on his way home to the reservation. They laid him in the back of their pickup truck, took him home, and sobered him up. Then they told him about the Saviour who could save him from all the demons as well as the white man's vices. They called on the *right* name. Harry's life verse became: "Neither is there salvation in any other; for there is no other name under heaven, given among men, whereby we must be saved" (Ac 4:12).

Back in our study in Mark's gospel, we soon came to the part about the two thousand pigs into which the demons went, followed by their being drowned in the sea. Harry's face clouded in puzzlement. Navajos do not keep pigs. Hopis do have a few—but two thousand of them! And drowning in the sea! This was too much. The largest body of water that Harry knew was a water hole on the reservation, not more than a half acre wide and not more than eighteen inches deep. You just could not drown two thousand pigs!

I went to my file and pulled out a picture of a hillside sloping down to the ocean shore and told Harry that there were many places in the world where there was that much water. Harry thought it over for a few moments and said, "That just like me, too!"

"How is that, Harry?"

He answered, "Well, Jesus came along and took the demon pig of drinking, the demon pig of gambling and fighting, the demon pig of bad women, and threw them all into the sea." He made a note of this in his little book and said, "I preach on that next Sunday." Harry had an early morning broadcast in the Navajo language, which he paid for himself. I listened to his next broadcast and, sure enough, he preached on the *bisoodi,* the pigs.

Harry continued to study and work and preach whenever he had an opportunity. Occasionally he would disappear for a week at a time when he could get off from his work. The first time he went away, unannounced, I was afraid that I had offended him in some way. When he returned as cheerful as ever, I asked him if I had said something that bothered him. He said, "No, I just had so much to tell my people that I went out on the reservation for a week." This was his habit from then on. His preaching area was his home clan in the southwestern corner of the reservation. The Santa Fe Railroad and Highway 66 bound the area on the south. Canyon Diablo runs through it from north to south, and the Little Colorado River runs along the north side of the area.

The family clan is the important kinship division of the population of the Navajo tribe, and practically all of the people in approximately two hundred square miles of area are related to Harry.

Harry was never able to attend the regular sessions of the school, but he came whenever he could take a few days or weeks off, such as when he had an accident that incapacitated him for a period of weeks.

In his cumulative studies, Harry became fluent in English and learned to read quite acceptably in both English and Navajo and could preach equally well in either. He is an excellent interpreter.

Things started to happen in the clan area. The crowd of relatives outgrew grandma's hogan, and a brush arbor was erected as the beginning of Harry's "campus," an area of about five acres. The area was in a natural depression sheltered by rimrock. A guest hogan was built where visiting Christians could live.

Harry somehow learned the word *indigenous* and established the Canyon Diablo Indigenous Church. A crudely lettered sign was erected by the trailside, where a dim trail led off through the desert to Harry's campus three miles away. If you are trying to find the Canyon Diablo church, turn off Highway 66 at the first turn after you have crossed the Canyon Diablo bridge, and go ten miles along the roughest roadway you have ever experienced. You will come to a water tank where several cattle trails merge. Turn to the left between the second and third Hereford steer and proceed into the desert. If you go more than three miles, you have taken the wrong cattle track.

Harry's cousins started gathering building materials from rubbish piles, abandoned sheds, an odd pile of boards donated by a lumberyard; and a building started taking shape. Walls were a composite of anything that could be nailed to the framework. The whole was covered with chicken wire; and stucco, made from native mud with a little cement mixed in, covered the outside wall. It looked neat when it was finished.

A discarded locomotive bell was scrounged from the Santa Fe and erected on the top of a piñon pole with a piece of haywire dangling to activate it.

They had no money for a cement floor, so they went over to the rimrock and pried out great slabs of colorful Arizona sandstone and laid a slab floor. It would be the envy of any architect. However, it is a little uncomfortable to kneel on in a long Navajo prayer meeting.

A furniture dealer donated three discarded davenports, all of which Harry placed on the platform. This is the only church I know where six visiting preachers can sit in overstuffed comfort waiting their turn to speak.

Spiritually things were happening as well. Young people, newly saved, started to enroll at Southwestern from Canyon Diablo. Graduated, they returned to the family clan to work with Harry. The rank and file started to learn to read their own language New Testaments. The brothers-in-law, whose prestige was in their own grandmother's clan area, started to move out and carry the message to areas that had never been reached. Several new churches were started, and a new set of students enrolled in the Bible Institute.

The Canyon Diablo Indigenous Church plays host to an annual camp meeting, where services will go on for three days at a time with sessions morning, afternoon, and evening. Guests camp in the compound under their wagons or in the bed of their pickups. Visitors who come from nearby camps will bring a sheep in the back of their pickup for a midday stew. Anything that is chewable will be put in the stew—Dried beans, potatoes, canned tomatoes. I saw one lady cutting up a green watermelon which probably added character to the stew. The women make great quantities of "fry-bread" which is fried in deep mutton fat and is delicious! Strong coffee fills out the menu.

Visitors, saved and unsaved, come from great distances. A few Hopi Christians attend from their mesas to the north. One always wishes, on returning from a Navajo camp meeting, that the church of Jesus Christ could experience the freedom and the heart warming ministry of such a gathering.

What does a service in a native Navajo church look like? I will describe the last one that I attended at Canyon Diablo. There is no printed program, of course, and the Holy Spirit has freedom to move on the hearts present. There is much singing. There does not have to be a musical instrument; in fact, such a device destroys some of the sweetness of the massed Navajo voices that are musical to begin with. Singing will continue for an hour or so at a time, and don't try to leave out any of the verses! The Navajos have their hymnbook memorized, and the nonliterates are confused if some verses are left out.

There will be prayer and testimonies and voluntary solos announced by the singer and not called for by the chairman. Several will give exhortations, and guests will be asked to express themselves.

There was one sister who had a great burden on her heart. She started to sing a hymn and broke down. She started to weep silently. Then she confessed that she had slipped from the way and wanted to get back in fellowship with the Lord. Everyone was so sympathetic and she confessed her sin publicly. All forgave her publicly and prayed for her. Finally, drying her tears, she told of her joy in being restored and then returned to her solo—all eight verses! The procedure took about an hour.

Another person, a middle-aged man, got up and made a brief announcement in Navajo and then started to read a chapter of Scripture, very stumblingly but persistently. He finally sat down with a satisfied smile. Everybody shared in his satisfaction. What was the occasion? He had just learned to read his Bible for himself, taught by one of the young graduates of the school, and this was his debut! He had mastered the art of reading his own language.

We watched another of our younger graduates performing. There was Lela Curley watching over the little ones. When they got too restless, she gathered them up—about twenty squirmers—and took them outside to a cozy nook under the rimrock, where she kept them quiet and busy for two solid hours. Lela has now married another graduate of the school, and they have started a new feature of the Navajo society—a Christian home. It is only a few years ago that Navajo marriages were arranged by parents, and often a Christian young person would be coerced into marrying a pagan because it was within the tribal pattern.

The story will end here for the moment. The pattern of the indigenous church is just emerging. New fires are being lit in many seemingly unlikely places. Missionary work by whites is diminishing, but now trained native leaders are being installed where there were white leaders a generation ago. The new work is emerging in the framework of the native society.

6

THE IMPORTANCE OF GRANDMOTHER

A little Navajo lady used to greet me at the trading post with a *ya-aat-eh* and a wisp of a smile. She was slender, wrinkled, her hair done in a knot on the back of her head, wearing a long-sleeved velvet bodice and flowing, many-pleated skirt, a turquoise and coral medallion at her throat, and Navajo moccasins with silver buttons showing beneath her skirt.

Then it came to me one day, that hers was one of the very-much-alike faces in my Monday night extension class. She always carried a Navajo New Testament that she could not read.

Ninety percent of the class spoke no English, so the classes were bilingual, with Scott Franklin interpreting.

One evening I announced that we would welcome them all at our Bible school. Scott promptly interpreted the message into Navajo. Little Grandmother's face brightened.

Within a matter of days, Grandmother appeared at

school with her Navajo New Testament in hand and a cotton sack of her personal belongings. She had come to learn to read her New Testament.

She had left the sheep for her daughters and grandchildren to tend. At the age sixty-five, she enrolled in school. Her name was Helen Littleman.

School was strange—so many people. She shared a dormitory room with a rather outgoing, buxom, Navajo woman who was the cook as well as a student.

She studied every moment that she was awake and was at the blackboard writing and sounding out the words at five in the morning. Her roommate encouraged and prodded her enthusiastically.

One semester was enough. She learned no English—she didn't want to—but by the end of the semester, she could read perfectly and could write freely with a beautiful hand.

She left as abruptly and as quietly as she had come. A ride in the back of the family pickup took her to the family clan area, where she promptly started to teach her daughters and grandchildren to read their own language.

The significance of the story is that it was the *grandmother* who went to all this effort. In the Navajo tribe, the succession is matrilineal. Grandmother is the esteemed head of the clan.

Grandmother (plus grandfather who belongs to another clan), her daughters, and their children constitute the nuclear family. The sons-in-law, like grandfather, belong to their own mothers' clans. The children in grandmother's camp are considered siblings.

The sons of grandmother have married into other

clans but still belong to her clan. The maternal uncles are the disciplinarians. Grandma's sons come back to her camp to discipline and teach their sisters' children.

It all seems confusing, but it seems to work perfectly in the Navajo society.

Incidentally, 58 percent of the world's native societies are matrilineal.

The women own the family sheep and the hogan and, of course, every woman and child from age three owns a horse. The men own their horses and saddles and usually the family pickup, if there is one.

The men own the religious rituals, which they have learned from their medicine-man uncles. The curing rites are conducted by the medicine men. These are learned by strenuous teaching from the time the boys are seven or eight until they become men.

It is quite natural for the men to take the lead in spiritual matters when they become Christian believers. The new church is set up in Grandmother's hogan!

7

OLD TIMERS

There are some glowing chapters in the story of the early missionaries who went to the Navajo tribe in the first two decades of the present century. These old timers are all gone, and another generation of missionaries has come and gone. Now native missionaries are taking over the field.

A few experiences have been handed down by word of mouth, and a few of the older Navajos will give snatches of tales of other days. But tragically, most of these devoted missionaries were too busy to keep diaries, and the stories were lost.

There was one exception. Howard Clark, a missionary of the Presbyterian church, laboring at Tolchoco, an almost unidentifiable spot on the Little Colorado River, kept a diary and prevailed upon his students to write their life stories.

There is mention of the journeys in company with other missionaries—Mitchell, Brink, Holcomb, Butler—and with native Christians who served as interpreters and preachers in their own native tongue—Manygoats, Curley, White Sheep, Sore Hip, and Big Water.

The following chapter is the story of an itineration by Clark and six of his Navajo associates as given in his faded diary loaned to me by his son, Dr. David Clark, of Riverside, California.

The trip was one of the first made by automobile in 1918, where nothing worthy of the name of road was present in an area of 25,000 square miles. Remember the ancient vehicles? Model T, Chevrolet 490, Overland? Shovels and a good supply of water were mandatory items in the supply kit.

One followed the few wagon tracks which often gave out at an abandoned sheep camp. Glen Girdner, the one remaining veteran of those days, tells of taking two weeks to cover two hundred miles with a Model T. He had to shovel sand most of the way. Several times the road was obliterated by flocks of sheep passing. It was then necessary to explore for a distance to find where the road continued.

Here is the story of one such missionary journey.

8

"I GO TO THE DESERT TO FIND MY SHEEP"

On Monday, June 18, at 7:15 A.M., in pursuance of our plan to evangelize the whole Navajo tribe, our party started for the northern section of the Navajo reservation, tributary to Shiprock and located on the San Juan River, this being the third trip of this kind. The following persons made up the party: Abraham Manygoats, native elder from Indian Wells Mission; Joe A-t se-di (Silver Smith), a convert of one year; Dineh Yazi, a man without feet who puts up two fingers when he speaks to show that he has been a Christian for two years; Howard Gorman, grandson of the famous William of Bath; Guy Clark, our native pastor at Ganado; and Wallace Silver Worker.

At Shiprock we were joined by Allen Nes-k'a hi, son of the fat medicine man; and Luke Johnson and Daniel Taylor, two of our students who have been loaned to that section for the summer to do evangelistic work.

Our first day's journey took us into four states. From

Ganado, Arizona, to Gallup, New Mexico; from Gallup by way of Shiprock into the southwest corner of Colorado; thence to Aneth, Utah, a total distance of over two hundred miles.

At this place we were bitten by hordes of mosquitoes and are still suffering from the poison with which they inoculated us. The crude trading post is carried on by a Mormon trader, being right on the bank of the San Juan River which flows into the Grand Colorado, above the Grand Canyon. The meeting for the morrow was announced to the stragglers at the store; and, having slept as best we could, next day we stretched our bed canvasses between the automobiles for a little shade from the burning sun, secured a sheep from a nearby camp, and prepared the "feed" of mutton stew, frying pan bread, and coffee; and preached the remainder of the day to the crowd which gathered.

As most of them knew nothing of God, it was a new experience to them, and they listened with great interest. At the close of the service, seeing some expression from the audience, they thanked us heartily for having come to them, and doubtless He who said: "Whatsoever a man soweth that shall he also reap," will bring some fruit from the sowing in this remote corner of the desert.

In the evening, we headed back to Shiprock, over fifty miles of perilous roads, formerly made by the early Mormon settlers, marked now by signs set up by the Indian who laid out our course for us. Cars being greased, gas tanks filled, we started again for a trip of 115 miles over a desolate country of rock and sand, the latter shifting wth the fierce winds that sweep across this desert. We stopped at Carriso Mountain, whose Navajo name indicates the long time it takes to pass it. We left word with the lonely trader that we would stop and talk to the Indians of this place upon our return. On again to the 55-mile point, Immanuel Mission, Salt Bush, where the Holcombs have their station and have been laboring faithfully for seven years without results. We tell them to gather the Indians and we will meet them upon our return. On again to the lonely trading post at Sweet Water. On again over the mountains of rock and great drifts of sand to where "The Big Rock Point" strikes out. Here is a lonely trading store. We tarry long enough to greet the trader and tell him the time of our return. Then on again for another thirty-five miles through a dreary land, enlivened now and then by curious rock formations sculptured by wind and sand, to the edge of Monument Valley which looks like a giant's playground, with its majestic forms of red sandstone, wrought out by nature and creating a feeling of awe in the observer.

The name of this place is Di-ne Ho-tsoh. It means "the last end of green things." Here are Navajo fields where they raise corn and melons. We are received at the lonely trading post by Jess Slalworthy, who is substituting for the trader gone with his family 120 miles to a sick relative. Jess gives us the run of the store, and, there being some hard ground free from loose sand within the enclosure, we make our camp, prepare supper, and announce our purpose to the Indians who drop around. Half-stewed mutton, greasy frying pan bread, and coffee three times a day, become tiresome, but it is "grub," and that's what we live on, with plenty of sand thrown in.

Jess gives us canned goods at wholesale prices and says we may use the "Bull Pen" for our meeting. This is the space inside the store in front of the counters, out of the way of drifting sand. We succeed in buying a lamb for seven dollars when they wanted nine for it, and while the feast is preparing, the gathering audience is herded into the store making a compact mass, with a few cross babies, and one after another, the members of the party shoot straight into their minds and hearts the old, old story of the Gospel, which is entirely new to them for they know nothing of God. The sun and the lightning are the highest deities to them.

There is not enough food prepared, so a new lot is put on to cook. While the meal is getting ready, the preaching continues late into the afternoon, making a day of it—just long enough to make the wonderful message penetrate into their dark minds and hearts, as it comes to them from their own color who know no word of English but who have by the power of the Holy Spirit come to know the language of heaven and can speak it with fervor.

When the time came to dismiss the people, they were asked what they thought of the message. They were shown their responsibility to accept and were asked to express their feelings in a definite way. If you want to walk in this new way, they were told, we will be glad to pray for you, and we invite you to take us by hand and give us your names that we may present them to God for the help of His Holy Spirit to lead you aright, to save you from hell, and to give you the knowledge of sins forgiven, and to make you partakers of heavenly blessing. In answer to this closing appeal, twenty-two persons signified their desire for help and gave us their names to be remembered in prayer. Among these were such names as His Arm, Big Water, Weaver, Sore Hip, Slim Red House, Singer's Sister, Curley Hair's oldest daughter, and White Sheep. Two of them were medicine men. Reader, will you not pray that the gracious message implanted in these hearts may, by the Holy Spirit, be quickened into new life?

In the hot sun of the following day, with boiling radiators, we plowed our way back to Rock Point and rested for a day in the shade of some cottonwood trees near the store. Then back to Holcombs where the Indians began to come in about the middle of the morning. By eleven o'clock in the cool basement with its earth floor, we had a good audience listening to the earnest presentation of the message by the various members of our party.

There were forty at this meeting, and, although many of them had been at an all night ceremony, they struggled against drowsiness to hear every word of the message, some leaning forward with great eagerness. As a result of the preaching, ten persons came forward, taking us by the hand and asking us to pray for them. This meeting was a great encouragement to the faithful workers who have labored here so long without results.

In the afternoon, back to Carriso then on to Shiprock, to a great heathen ceremony where between four and five hundred gaily dressed heathen Indians were gathered under the leadership of a medicine man called Fat Man's Son, father of Rev. Campbell's interpreter. This medicine man is an unusual character. He is of the leonine type and looks as if, given our opportunities, he might have been a judge on the supreme bench. Genial mannered and cordial, he invited us to eat and gave us opportunity to witness for Christ to the gathered Indians. An unaccustomed visitor to this scene would be fascinated by so many fine physical specimens of humanity, sitting straight up on their horses, decked in "ten gallon" hats, massive silver belts, booted and spurred, and wearing the brightest colors that can be purchased at the trading stores; the women too in bright colors with a profusion of silver ornaments made from our American money. It is a gripping scene, but they are ignorant of God and His salvation.

Bunching our automobiles and turning on the headlights, the cornet played by one of our number drew the crowd together. We read and sang one of our Navajo hymns, and the first speaker stepped forward, telling what Christ had done for him and would do for them. And so on until all had spoken earnestly. As we looked into the fine faces of those young men crowded about us, showing out clearly in the glare of the headlights, how we coveted them for Christ and how glad we were, when, at the close of the service and the invitation was given, some of them came forward to give us their names and ask that we remember them in prayer.

Among this number was the greatest medicine man himself who had already been impressed by the conversion of his son. What a power he could be among his people if the saving grace of God should come into his life and heart! You will surely offer prayer for him and for the others who need our help so much.

After eight days of this work, it is good to turn our faces homeward from greasy tin pans, sandy food and soiled dishcloths, and hard beds to a bathtub, and to put one's feet under a table and eat home cooking again, and to have abiding joy that comes with the knowledge that the message of heaven has been carried to needy souls, and to know that Christ is glorified and that God will give the increase.

This trip covered 735 miles and cost us about seventy dollars for food and gasoline. Other sections of this great field are asking our help, and we must keep it up.

9

NAVAJO BIBLE

During the first decade of the present century, some arduous attempts were made by missionaries of the Christian Reformed church and the Presbyterian church to reduce the Navajo language to writing and to translate at least some key portions of the Scriptures. The first Scriptures to be printed in the language were the Gospel of Mark and the book of Genesis. L. P. Brink of the Christian Reformed church translated the portions which were printed by the American Bible Society.

These early translators did not have the advantage of the skills later developed by the Wycliffe Translators, but they produced much trial material which paved the way for the more accurate translation of the New Testament in 1956 and the Old Testament, which is in the final stages of preparation as this is being written.

An interesting story is given in the diaries of the Reverend Howard Clark, one of the Presbyterian missionaries. It is worth recording.

One day a missionary (probably Clark himself), having saddled his horse, tied his blankets on behind, put a little lunch in the saddle pocket for the first day at noon, said good-bye to the home folks, started out on a fifty-mile trip to last five days. As he rode over the barren waste skirting the river, he was asking God to make a way for the truth and to help him make it plain. Nine miles out, he climbed the face of the mesa and found himself straining his eyes along the course of the road for twenty miles as it traced its way through the vast expanse of the painted desert, to where great mesas of bright red sandstone formed a line stretching down the river to the north for sixty miles.

As he was about to drop off his horse, he saw a black speck in the distance and knew instinctively that it was a Navajo horseman. By the time the horse was hobbled to pick up a little grass and the missionary had settled down in the shade of a greasewood bush to eat his lunch, the rider came plainly into view and in a very short time was seated under the same bush sharing the lunch.

"Where are you going?" asked the native.

"I am going to the Lakes," replied the missionary.

"What are you going to do up there?"

"You know what I am going to do. I am going to tell the Good News."

"It is no use to go up there now; this week they are having a big singing ceremony over the wife of Tsi-des-giz-ni Yazi, and all the people are going to that."

The missionary's heart sank for a moment; then faith revived with the thought of the way Christian overcame Appollyon. He said, "I will at least improve the present opportunity," and proceeded to tell Zaha all he could of the Gospel with his limited knowledge of the Navajo.

Then he went forward pleading the word from the Book, "Greater is He that is in you than he that is in the world."

The first night was spent at the camp of Dona-gahi (the man who cannot walk). They killed a sheep so that the missionary might have some meat. One of the family, in cutting up the fat in which the liver was to be fried, found the knife rather dull so he used his teeth.

When supper was over and the firelight was gleaming on the red faces in the circle, the old old story was told to them to the best of the missionary's ability. Then a chief present, Dinah Yazi, who had heard the Gospel many times, supplemented the imperfect presentation by telling all he knew about it.

Next day Ja-di-hi-i's place was visited, where the same thing occurred again, Chief Diney Yazi being present.

At the close of the talk, the chief said, "Why do you not go down to where the ceremony is being held, they are resting today and will listen to you." Taking the suggestion as from the Lord, the missionary went to the camp of Tsi-des-giz-ni Yazi, and was cordially greeted by the medicine man in charge and given a sheepskin on which to recline next to him and near the patient.

The sick woman, about fifty years of age, was doubtless suffering from indigestion as a result of much coffee and frying-pan bread, but the medicine man, having inquired into the family history, decided it was because just before the patient was born fifty years ago, her mother had seen two bears killed, and now the spirits of these bears were giving her all her trouble.

The method of treatment was to make a big fire in the middle of the hogan. Men and women, all stripped to the waist were then made to perspire so freely that the sweat ran off them. Then an emetic weed being bruised in water was administered to the patient and all present, except the medicine man. Thus with everybody helping the patient to throw off the evil spirits, it was evident to her that she would have relief. The practitioner waved his sacred feathers, driving out the spirits, and outside, where they must pass, was a bouquet of flowers and feathers and a pan of meal for their comfort and that they might be appeased for being driven out.

As it was rest day, all seemed pleased to have the missionary come, and after the news had been told, he drew from his pocket the manuscript Gospel of Mark; turning to the story of the man of Gadara, he read to the company of men and women in their own language of Him who had power to cast out the legion of devils. It is needless to say that the audience was spellbound by the reading of this record which was so appropriate to the occasion and so suited to their needs.

The missionary was given a very forceful illustration of the fact that the old Book is right up to date for every people in every age.

When the reading and comments were finished, the impressive silence was broken by the medicine man himself, usually the strongest opponent of the Gospel which will release the people from his power. He said, "My friends, I have often thought there was something lacking in our Navajo religious system; surely this book from which our younger brother has read to us this story is very truth."

Because the Lord had proved Himself stronger than Satan and had given signal manifestation of it all along the way, the missionary turned his willing horse homeward with a song of triumph in his heart and upon his lips.

10

ABRAHAM MANYGOATS

Abraham Manygoats has become a legend on the Navajo reservation.* The last time he was seen in Flagstaff was in 1963, when he strode up the long lane of the Mt. Elden Bible Conference grounds, his pack on his back, as he had done almost every year for half a century.

He stayed for the two week conference, totally deaf, but surrounded by the scenes of other days, when he had been the intimate of some of the greatest Bible teachers of the century—Gaebelein, Ironside, Pettengill, Armerding, and others. It was still the same here under the pines, and yet, with his old friends all gone, it wasn't the same. He returned to the reservation with the feeling that it was time for him to go too, and, the last time we heard, he had marched triumphantly, at age one hundred, with his Stetson hat and his silver-buckled moccasins, right up to the pearly gates.

*This story is adapted from the author's book, *No Dark Valley* (Flagstaff, Ariz.; Southwestern School of Missions Press, 1965).

We come across references to him in the diaries of some of the great missionaries to the Navajos—Howard Clark, Fred Mitchell, Horace Holcomb. We find him as the preaching partner of these men, back in the 1920s, laboring hundreds of miles from his own community. We see much of him built into the lives of native preachers whose ministries were enriched by his patriarchal counsel.

Besides having many goats, he had many descendents, and it is quite common to run across individuals who say, "Oh, he was my grandfather." Among them is Scott Franklin, one of the most stolid of the present-day Navajo preachers.

On one occasion some of his friends thought it would be interesting to take this simple native back East to see the big cities with their towering buildings. Manygoats was not particularly impressed, except by the utter silliness of apparently normal human beings encrusting the soft earth with brick and cement that wore out one's moccasins, and building their huge "hogans" up to the sky like the Tower of Babel.

They say that he preached an eloquent sermon on one of the street corners in the Chicago Loop. He told the crowds to flee from the wrath to come before their great piles of brick and stone tumbled around their heads when God would shake this wicked earth in His judgment.

One of his illustrations has been used by preachers around the world in many versions. I like the local version best. Dr. H. A. Ironside was discussing the subject of the two natures in the believer and asked

Manygoats to give his own experience in the matter. Manygoats explained the experience this way: "Before I became a Christian, a black dog lived inside my heart. Then one day Jesus came and saved me. Then a white dog came in my heart. Before the white dog came everything all quiet. After I was saved, black dog and white dog fight. White dog on top, everything all right; black dog on top everything go wrong."

Dr. Ironside then asked him how he resolved the situation. He replied: "Feed white dog."

11

LIFE STORY OF ABRAHAM MANYGOATS

When I was a little boy, I remember distinctly that my father, mother, brothers, and sisters were in constant fear of raiding parties, particularly the Utes from the north, the Apaches and Mexicans from the south, and the Zuni and Pueblo from the east. These war parties would kill our people, drive off our stock, and carry us into captivity.

My people were also afraid of many things, such as the bear, the owl, and the numberless evil spirits supposed to infest the air and bring upon us the ills of life, sickness, and other misfortunes. Especially were they afraid of the witchcraft practiced by evil-minded Navajos who go about in coyote skins (the wolf-skin people, a demonistic cult), and shoot into people such missiles as white beads, cartridges made of charcoal, and coyote whiskers.

The first white people I ever saw were some Mormons who came through the country, some of them settling near us at Tuba, Arizona. I am told that these were with John D. Lee who took refuge in the wilds of our Navajo country following the Mountain Meadows Massacre. My early home was near Tuba at a place called the Lakes.

The first I ever heard of school was from a Pah Ute slave among our Navajo people. He told us a school was being started at Tuba. My people all thought that they would not want to send their children to school because they might get sick and die away from home.

When I was fifteen years of age, I made a trip of one hundred-fifty miles across the country to the place I now live, called Indian Wells. I paid a lot of horses for a wife, and, after living with her about a year, I went back to my own people. When I was nearly thirty years of age, I again left home, this time on account of the scarcity of water, grass, and food. I married again at Indian Wells and have lived there ever since.

The first time I ever heard of God must be about twenty years ago. A man with gold in his teeth came near where I lived. He was driving a couple of burros packed with his food and bedding. He knew a little of the Navajo language, so made us understand that all who did not believe on God's Son, who died on the cross, were God's enemies and could never go to heaven.

Six years later I went to Tolochaco, and there I learned more of the Gospel from Mr. Johnston, the missionary there. Then later Mr. Schwab came as the missionary to Indian Wells, and I heard the same story again from him. When Mr. Schwab left, Mr. Johnston and his family came to take up the work at Indian Wells. As I was often at the mission, I began to believe the Gospel, but I did not give up any of my Navajo ways. I went to all the ceremonies and dances; I gambled and did everything else to divert my mind from my sinful condition and my need of the Saviour. I was like a man suffering from thirst who could find nothing to satisfy that inner craving.

Since Mr. Ward and family came, I have really accepted the Gospel, and now I know the Lord Jesus Christ as my personal Saviour. My heart has, at last, found rest and peace. My fifty-four years of sinning have been wasted, but now I am in the fold. Now I am not afraid of owls, evil spirits, and medicine men, or even death; I am afraid only of sin. Even in my sleep I am afraid of sin, for when I dream now of using tobacco or whiskey or of practicing impurity, I seem to remember that I have given all that up and shrink back from the least suggestion of it.

Now I can see the gracious hand of God in so many things. Last fall I went to work at Leupp for a time. I supposed, of course, that the corn I had stored would be all gone when I returned, but I found it had not been touched. I am sure that God took care of it for me.

We had a very cross overseer where I worked; he would discharge some Indians almost every day, but he was never cross to Luke or myself. The range around Indian Wells has, for years, been infested with loco, which poisons the stock; and now it has disappeared. Surely my heavenly Father did this for me because I am serving Him.

Before I was saved, I felt like an old man but now

I feel quite young. I felt I was getting old very fast, for my shoulders ached, my legs ached. Now I do not think there is a young man around here who feels any more lively than I do. I race and wrestle with the young fellows in the Bible school at Ganado. I am learning to read the Scriptures in my own language so that then I can go out and tell the wonderful story to my own people who are still in darkness. I, who once was a medicine man and very deep in sin, am now a child of God, saved and kept by the power of God.

Now, Howard Clark will take up Abraham's story from his point of view.

When, upon a certain occasion, I was administering the sacrament of the Lord's Supper at Indian Wells, I noticed Abraham Manygoats taking the communion. As I had known him for many years as a typical heathen, I was surprised, so I interviewed him after the service. I asked him if he was a Christian, and he said yes. "How long have you been saved?" I asked. He said, "About one month ago." I then asked him if he had given up his Navajo prayers and ceremonies. He replied that he had. "Have you really turned your back on the whole system?" I enquired. He said yes. Then someone asked him what he thought of the old way, and, after thinking a moment, he said, "It is about like a dead horse that you can smell for a mile."

When I was requested by the women's board to bring Spot-of-whiskers-on-his-chin, now called William Gorman, to the general assembly at Winona Lake, I sent word to the effect that his home was at Chin Lee, Arizona, but he had to hunt up some lost cattle and could not come. In this crisis, my mind turned to Manygoats, so I went to Indian Wells to see if he would accompany me. Going to his camp in the morning, I found him at breakfast and told him of my errand. After he considered the matter a few minutes, he put his hand up to the back of his head and said, "I fear that my hair is not according to the Word of God." The superstitious fears of his family had kept him from having it cut. I advised him to leave it as it was until he returned so that he would not be embarrassed by the change when he was among strangers. His first visit to civilization was immensely interesting to him, and his testimony concerning God's transforming grace was an inspiration to all who heard it.

12

KICKAPOO

Mention the Kickapoo, and small boys start to chuckle. They know only Hairless Joe and his buddy in the Al Capp comic strip, and their favorite beverage, "Kickapoo Joy Juice."

The Kickapoo are mentioned in association with the Siwash and the Diggers. The facts are that there were no such tribes as the Siwash and Diggers. The Kickapoo, on the other hand, are a very noble tribe of the Algonkian language family who lived in prehistoric times on the south shore of Lake Ontario in what is now New York state. They moved west as the Hokan tribes (Iroquois) moved north to Lake Ontario and over into Canada.

One band of the Kickapoo live today in Coahuila state in Mexico and have retained, to a large degree, the life-style of their ancestors in pre-Columbian days. Other bands live in Oklahoma and Kansas.

And Kickapoo "joy juice" is no joke. Crying Wind, one of our Kickapoo correspondents, gives the following recipe:

1 quart raw alcohol
1 pound rank black chewing tobacco
1 bottle Jamaica ginger
1 handful red peppers
1 quart black molasses
1 quart water

Mix well. Simmer until all the strength is drawn from the tobacco and peppers and drain.

Crying Wind explains, "That recipe may explain why there are so few Kickapoo left."

13

WALTER KASKUSKE

He reached for the handrail on the moving freight car—and missed. A severed leg landed him in the hospital.

This seemed like the end of the trail for Walter Kaskuske, a fifty-year-old Kickapoo Indian with a third-grade education, a typical situation in America.

Walter had spent his many years since young manhood nomading around the United States as a crop worker and odd-jobs man. Sometimes he was with small bands of his own people; sometimes he lived as a "lone wolf." The home reservation was poorly situated and quite inadequate to supply the needs of the tribe. They became migrant workers, with an annual return to the home reservation.

Ken Antone, an Oneida Indian Christian, visited Walter in the hospital and told him that Jesus, the Son of the Most High God, whom the tribe knew from antiquity, had died for the sins of mankind, including Indians. Walter knew about God whom the Kickapoo worshiped as the Master of Life, and he knew about the

Great Spirit who ruled over the lives of men, but he did not know that Jesus was God's son who had died for his sins. He thought *Jesus* was just a white man's swear word.

This was a tremendous revelation to Walter, and as Ken read the word of God and explained the great fact of the incarnation and the plan of salvation, Walter grasped it greedily. Now there seemed to be something in life, even for a middle-aged Kickapoo with a wooden leg.

Two carloads of Kickapoo folks arrived the next summer at the all-Indian Bible conference under the pines at Flagstaff, Arizona. They had come all the way from Oklahoma accompanied by their missionary, Ken Antone.

They were obviously poor in this world's goods but were possessed of a quiet and serene dignity that well befitted their tribal heritage. The men wore nondescript and unmatched suits or overalls, and the women wore Quakerish looking dresses (the Kickapoo had been assigned to Quaker overseers in 1870). They wore white kerchiefs on their heads and tied under their chins.

The Kickapoo were quite in contrast to the colorful Seminoles in their intricately embroidered blouses and skirts worn by both men and women. The Seminole had come all the way from Florida with their leader, Billy Osceola.

The Kickapoo had only recently been introduced to solid Bible teaching and were rejoicing as worshiping believers in their quiet way.

With them was a new believer, Walter, still a bit unsteady on his artificial leg but possessed of a spirit of wonder and expectancy in this new orbit in which he was traveling. The old habitat of the fruit-picking camps and the hobo jungle were far away.

Bible school was proposed to Walter. But how could a middle-aged Indian with a third-grade education ever expect to fit into such a picture? Then he met other middle-aged Navajos, Hopis, and Hualapais with educations as limited as his, actually making satisfactory grades in Bible school. The element in their lives that made them succeed was their united love for the Lord Jesus and their desire to know all they could about His Word. Fall saw him hobbling up to school from the bus depot with his little bag of belongings.

The new life that now possessed him made him attack his assignments with stolid persistence. He earned consistent if not high grades through his three years at Southwestern. One thing was always noticed: he read his Bible faithfully and showed a deep devotion and attachment to his Saviour.

It was always a benediction to hear him in prayer. What had captivated him was that this Son of the Most High God had loved him enough to die for him. He would always close his prayer in an awed and almost inaudible voice, "In the name of Thy Son, Amen."

Walter's appreciation of the fact of the incarnation was most gratifying. A look at the religious history of the Kickapoos shows that they were never a pagan tribe in the true sense of the word. They were noted by the celebrated portrait painter of the Indians, George Catlin, as holding a day of the week sacred with the active worship of the Most High God. Small engraved paddles were used as reminders of the progress of the petitions. The medicine man was conspicuously absent in the Kickapoo society.

On one occasion a missionary from Africa spoke in chapel at the Bible school each day. He was emphasizing the fact that the Africans were idolators and that they were, in their more sordid rituals, worshiping evil spirits. The missionary then included the American Indians in the practice of such worship. Walter was highly offended and stalked from the room, his stride emphasized by his wooden leg.

He did not return to any of the good missionary's talks. He explained to me, "Our people were never idolators, and we had no spirit worship among us. Our prophet [Kanakuk] was a true man of God and led our people away from the wickedness of the white men."

Each year at the close of the school year, Walter would disappear to look in the fruit camps for his tribe. He became their traveling missionary, earning his own way. He would usually report by means of a picture postcard, reading somewhat as follows: "Found my band camped under the International bridge at McAllan, Texas. See you in the fall." This was a quite satisfactory field report from a missionary.

Walter had his mind well made up long before he was through with his three years in school. He would be a missionary. The Kickapoos were divided into three bands, one each in Kansas and Oklahoma, and one in Old Mexico, where they had gone over a hundred years ago to avoid going on an undesirable reservation and to escape involvement in the Civil War. Walter would go to this band.

At graduation, Walter told me of his aims. We sought to help him by asking about his material needs. How would he get to the field? His thumb had carried him around the U.S. in the old days; it would still serve to get him to the mission field. What about his outfit? He had good work clothes; he would wear them to his field. How about support on the field? His reply pointed to the very core of the idea of indigenous missions. He said, "I will join my tribe in Mexico; I will build a shelter and get a mule and a plow. I will plant a garden like the others and I will be their shepherd." He would not need a furlough fund; he was an indigenous missionary, living quietly and ministering to his flock at home on the mission field.

Language school was no problem. Walter was already bilingual, English and Kickapoo. For practical purposes, living in Mexico, he acquired Spanish.

14

KICKAPOO THEISM

The Kickapoo, like many of the American tribes, knew the Most High God and worshiped Him in a completely devout manner.

They did not know of the incarnation for the simple reason that they were in America before the birth of Christ in Bethlehem.

Many of the tribes knew of the Most High as the Creator and Sustainer but thought of Him as so remote from the affairs of earth and earth people that He was no longer interested in their worship.

It is among these latter that localized superstitious rituals were developed to appease or exorcise the evil spirits that bothered them. Among village-dwelling tribes, such as the Pueblos, group rituals developed that were practiced by the tribe as a whole. In nomadic tribes the rituals were not prominent, but in these tribes, shamans or medicine men appeared as specialists who would exorcise an evil spirit or effect a cure for a fee.

Unfortunately the missionaries saw only the sordid forms of religious ritual and concluded that the Indians were without any concept of God. They proceeded to establish the idea that the white men were the only ones who knew about God and proceeded to instruct the Indians accordingly.

Had the missionaries waited until they found out what the Indians really believed and then had they told them that their Most High God had sent His Son to die for their sins, they would have been successful in their efforts. In the few cases where missionaries took this approach, the tribes became Christian in a remarkably short time. The Indians were still waiting for a Messiah.

Ritzenthaler and Peterson tell us:

> The Kickapoo believe in a supreme being called Kichia 'Ta who dwells in the sky and who is believed to have created earth and all things on the earth. The Kickapoo believe that their God takes a special interest in them and follows the very doings of each person.
>
> The Kickapoo are tolerant toward other religions and are constantly pointing out that their God is the same as that of the Christian and other religions. They say that their religion and Christianity are very similar in teaching good conduct, such as the avoidance of theft, murder, lying and dishonor. They point out, however, that while the Kickapoo practise their ethics, people of other religions, especially the Christians, often do not.*

*Robert E. Ritzenthaler and Frederick A. Peterson, *The Mexican Kickapoo Indians* (Milwaukee: Milwaukee Public Museum Publ. in Anthropology, 1956), p. 46. The *Kichia' Ta* of the Kickapoo is the equivalent of the *Kitchee Manito* of other Algonkians. The *Ta* is the universal morpheme indicating the name of the God of heaven. Thus, *Kichia* (great) *Ta* (God).

The Kickapoo always gave thanks before eating and offered the first fruits each season to the Most High before partaking of the fruit themselves. The thanksgiving feast is almost universal among the American tribes; and, wherever it is held, it is always in honor of the Most High.

The Kickapoo considered themselves always under the scrutiny of God. Kanakuk, the Kickapoo prophet, in his address to General William Clark in St. Louis in 1831, said,

> "My father, everytime we eat we raise our hands to the Great Spirit to give us success. . . .
>
> My father, we are sitting by each other here to tell the truth. If you write anything wrong the Great Spirit will know it. If I say anything not true the Great Spirit will hear it.
>
> Everything belongs to the Great Spirit. If He chooses to make the world shake, or turn it over, all the skins, white and red, cannot stop it. I have done. I trust the Great Spirit."†

George Catlin, the celebrated artist who made a portrait of Kanakuk, the prophet, observed that the Kickapoo were devout in their attendance at worship.‡ They had a meeting each Friday in which they confessed their sins and on Sunday had a public worship service.

Kanakuk had prepared small wooden paddles for each worshiper, which were carved with mnemonic de-

†James Mooney, *Fourteenth Annual Report of the Bureau of Ethnology* (Washington, D.C.: Government Printing Office, n.d.), 2:695.

‡Ibid, pp. 695, 699.

vices as an aid in remembering the sequence of the prayer requests. The prayers were uttered in unison.

Catlin assumed that the Kickapoo were merely imitating the Christians, but the records fail to reveal any Christian contacts. The only missionary contact was with Isaac McCoy in Iowa and that only briefly. In 1830 a delegation of Kickapoo visited with the Reverend James Armstrong who gave them New Testaments.

The Quaker missionaries who were assigned to the Kickapoo band in Oklahoma in 1870 seemed totally occupied with teaching them to farm and to educate them in English and other useful arts and crafts.

15

CRYING WIND

The story of Crying Wind is that of a little girl who lived in two native culture areas, the Kickapoo in Kansas and the Navajo in Arizona. Her father was a Navajo. She acquired the traits of each; but, since native Americans have a matrilineal kinship pattern, she was brought up with an emphasis on the Kickapoo heritage. She knows and reads the Navajo language.

Crying Wind experienced the impact of the white man's culture in high school and college and knows only too well the pressures of a native American adjusting to employment in the city. But let her tell her own story.

* * *

My blood is Kickapoo, Navajo, and white; but since my Grandmother was Kickapoo, it is that tribe we claim.

Grandmother Pearl Cadue was bought by a half-breed, my grandfather, for a cigar box half-full of nickles, when she was fourteen. This was on the Kickapoo reservation near Horton, Kansas, in 1907.

They had eleven children and raised them in the old ways. I was taught these old ways by my mother.

I cannot remember a time I did not worship the wind, though we called him Níyol (the Navajo word for wind). I live in constant fear of him, because who can escape the wind? He is always here day or night, summer or winter. When the wind cried at night (regardless of time or temperature), I would take a prayer stick, run to the nearest hill, draw a *yeibitche* symbol in the dust, and beg the wind for mercy (or strength), and throw the prayer stick into the wind, and quickly turn my back, because to see the stick fall meant the prayer would be unanswered. Grandma said the *yeibitche* symbol was to help get the prayer up over the mountains and halfway to the moon, where the wind would be able to hear it.

Death was even more frightening than life. Once someone died, you were given three days to inform people; and, after that, the dead person's name was not to be spoken aloud for a year. To do so would call them back from the dead, and they would stay with you forever. On the anniversary of the death, it was always necessary to burn cedar in the house (cedar smoke kept away dead spirits), because once a year that person would return at night asking to be welcomed home.

My family—grandmother, my parents, seven uncles, and others—lived close together. There was a lot of stealing, fighting, and drunkenness in the family, as they worshiped the old gods and argued among themselves. As I said before, I was deeply dedicated to the wind and had no idea of what any other god would be like. After I moved away from home to get work in a city, I found myself completely alone. I had no friends, my family was back home, there was no one I could even talk to.

The city was a hard place for an Indian to be; I missed the trees and the soft earth. Here there were only buildings and cement. The wind in the city streets seemed different than the wind back in the mountains.

Often at night, I would walk out to the edge of the city to some hills and climb up to the top of them where I knew Indians had sat a thousand years ago and prayed to my same god. I would sit there in the dust and wait for the wind to come to speak to me; sometimes the wind would talk, sometimes it would not.

I told a woman at work that I was lonely, and she said to talk to a minister. I didn't know any ministers; but that night, alone in my room, I picked up the telephone book and opened to the yellow pages and picked a name at random and called a minister. I was surprised when he said he would come to see me that same night.

I was very nervous and afraid that this man would laugh at what I told him. But he didn't laugh. He just sat there and listened to what I had to say, and very quietly he told me a little about a stronger God than mine. I wasn't very interested in another God; I was having enough trouble with the god I already had.

He invited me to eat dinner with his family, which I did almost every night for the next few weeks. I was always surprised at how peaceful his family was—no fights in this house. They always made me feel welcome. I knew I was spending too much time at their house, but I was so lonely I didn't make the effort to stay away. They never preached to me, although they would sometimes mention how God had done this or that. It was many months before I was brave enough to attend church with them on a Sunday morning. I was so scared! I'd never been inside of a church and I didn't know what to expect. It was very quiet. The soft organ music was a welcome change from the harsh drum beats I was used to. The people were friendly, and so I returned again and again.

I made no effort to change my beliefs. I still believed in the old ways, but I was becoming more and more empty inside. One night I heard the wind calling me outside, and I went back to the hills. I used my prayer stick and asked the wind to speak to me. There was nothing. The wind was gone. I needed help, but the wind was someplace blowing down some other valley. I knew I was alone on that hill. I knew I had always been alone, and I was afraid.

It was the middle of the night when I reached the minister's house and banged on his door. They got out of bed and welcomed me inside. If they had said to come back the next morning, I would have killed myself. I'd been thinking a lot about suicide lately. They sat up the rest of the night talking to me about Jesus, and before dawn I turned my back on the wind and accepted Christ as my Saviour. There was light in my life, and fear was gone.

As I look back, I can see how God worked in my life and how He directed me to that particular minister who was sympathetic and understanding.

Shortly after I joined the church, I was standing on a street corner waiting for a light to change, and in the gutter lay a piece of paper with Navajo written on it. I was really surprised to see Navajo words, so I picked it up and read it. It had some scripture and the address of a mission in Arizona. I took the paper home and wrote to the mission. They answered and said they knew a mission in New Mexico that needed helpers. I wrote to that mission, and in two weeks found myself on a bus headed down there to help them for the summer. I ended up staying for a couple of years. I had seven dollars in my pocket when I got on that bus and made the five-hundred-mile trip to the mission that I had never heard of before. God had planned things for me, and it was a happy time in my life.

* * *

Crying Wind is now married and has two little boys, Aaron and Shane. The family lives on a farm in Oklahoma.

Crying Wind is also an artist and a writer. She has managed to retain her native handcrafting. She knows the art of curing deer skin and elk hides and has a garment of her own handwork made from two elk hides beautifully adorned with beads in true Kickapoo fashion.

16

WHO ARE THE KICKAPOO?

Dim tradition has the Kickapoo and their cousin tribes, the Sauk and Fox, originating as a segment of the Algonkian language family, living on the south shore of Lake Ontario. They were hunters and gatherers and probably cultivated corn after that plant was introduced from the south.

At some unknown time, probably one or more centuries before Columbus arrived, a wedge of migrating Hokan tribes pushed north into Algonkian country. The tip of the wedge penetrated to the shore of Lake Ontario and later across that lake into Canada. The Huron tribe, a member of the Hokan family, moved into Ontario and occupied lands reaching west to Lake Huron. They were cultivators of corn and tobacco. These Hokan tribes came to dominate the territory and were called Iroquois by the French.

Before the coming of the whites into the territory, the Iroquois, or Six Nations, were well organized into a league of nations. In the history of the Northeastern states and Quebec, the Iroquois tribes were allies of the

English, and the Algonkian tribe sided with the French. What is known in history as the French and Indian Wars were rather French and English wars with the Algonkians and Iroquois pitted against each other and doing the nastiest fighting.

The Kickapoos, always a peaceful tribe, moved west, along the base of the Great Lakes in company with the Saux and Fox. The first historic note places them in Wisconsin. As Ritzenthaler and Peterson tell us,

> While not recorded as being in Wisconsin in 1634 by Nicolet, the first explorer of that area, the Kickapoo with their close cultural and linguistic affiliates, the Sauk and Fox, were noted as occupants of Central Wisconsin some twenty years later. It is possible that they were there and not contacted by Nicolet, but it seems more probable that these groups were driven into the area by Iroquois pressure, arriving during the first half of the 17th century, and apparently moving in from the south along the south shore of Lake Michigan. The Kickapoo were reported by Allouez, in about 1667-70, as occupying an area near the portage of the Fox and Wisconsin rivers in south central Wisconsin, in what would now be Columbia County. They were not a large tribe, early estimates of their numbers ranging from 2000 to 3000. By 1720, they had also ranged into northern Illinois as far as the Illinois River, and they and the Mascoutens were described by Charlevoix (pp. 269-271) as the sole inhabitants of this and their southern Wisconsin territory.
>
> With the destruction of the Illinois Confederacy by the combined efforts of the southern Wisconsin tribes, about 1765, the Kickapoo, Sauk, and Fox were

awarded lands left vacated by the confederacy tribes, and left Wisconsin. Some of the Kickapoo settled around Peoria extending their range south to center around the Sagamon River, and became known as the "Prairie band," while another group split off moving eastward to settle on the Wabash and Vermillion rivers, where they became known as the "Vermillion band." Their fifty odd years of residence in Illinois saw the rise of Kenekuk, the famous Kickapoo prophet, and the War of 1812 in which the Kickapoo sided with the British. During this period also, one group voluntarily emigrated to Indian Territory.

After the war came the development of the removal policy under President Monroe (1817-1825) and his Secretary of War, John C. Calhoun. Designed to move all tribes west of the Mississippi River, this policy had almost immediate effect upon the destiny of the Kickapoo. On July 30, 1819, the Prairie band, and a month later the Vermillion band, signed treaties relinquishing their rights to 13,000,000 acres of land in the Illinois-Indiana area, and accepting a tract in southwestern Missouri. The movement of the Kickapoo to their new home began the same year, but difficulties arose as some of the Indians refused to leave. The removal was accomplished over the next four years, however, and by 1824 there were 2,200 Kickapoo living at their new home on the Osage River.

The Plains Phase

In Missouri new problems arose. Difficulties with the Osage over hunting rights, and the moving in of white squatters on their sixty-mile-square territory, created almost daily incidents which influenced the

Kickapoo, in 1831, to petition for a new reservation in Kansas. In 1832 this petition was granted, and in the following year they began moving to their new reserve, a tract of 1200 square miles near Fort Leavenworth in the northeastern corner of Kansas. This settlement has survived to modern times, with the United States Indian Bureau reporting a population of 343 in 1940, although the question has been raised as to how many of these are actually Potawatomi rather than Kickapoo. Indications are that not all moved to Kansas with Kenekuk in 1833, but that a group split off and settled in Texas.

Some in the Kansas band were successful farmers, while another segment preferred hunting. In 1837 a few hundred of the latter group set off on a hunting expedition to Texas, where they joined up with the other Kickapoo band, and never returned to Kansas. In 1838 there was a reported population in Kansas of 724.

The Kickapoo seem to have been in the area which became Texas for a considerable length of time. Around 1775, they were granted a concession of land by the King of Spain, Charles III, in exchange for their services in keeping out some of the marauding southern Plains tribes (Fabila, p. 25). In February, 1778, the Kickapoo chief was called to New Orleans and presented with a silver medal by the Spanish Viceroy in reward for this policing aid provided by the tribe (Fabila, p. 25). This medal is said to be still in the possession of the Mexican Kickapoo.

The Texas band established a permanent village on their land grant, and in 1824 had an estimated population of 800, which was augmented in 1837 by the arrival of several hundred from the Kansas band.

Texas, after declaring its independence from Mexico in 1836, honored the Spanish land grants of the Kickapoo. However, trouble with Mexico was still brewing and Texas, fearful that the Kickapoo would side with Mexico in the event of further hostilities, finally, in 1839, forced them to leave. They entered Indian Territory settling in central Oklahoma along the Canadian River and adjacent to Friendly Creek. Around 1858, they were joined by a group of the Kansas band under the leadership of the prophet Kenekuk.

It should be noted that the main contacts and associations of the Kickapoo during their Plains phase were with other Woodland tribes, especially the Potawatomi and Shawnee, and their culture was and is almost totally unaffected by Plains culture.

The Mexican Phase

In 1850 a delegation of Oklahoma Kickapoo and Seminole, under the leadership of the Seminole chief, Wild Cat, journeyed to Mexico City to petition for land in that country. An audience with President Herrera resulted in their being granted a section for colonization in return for their promise to aid in checking the Indian raids along the border.

An agreement was signed by the Inspector of Colonies on June 27, 1850, in which the tribes were given four sites of land near Morelos, Coahuila, equal to those which the government usually gave for military colonies, to be held in perpetuity. Wild Cat was named as chief of the combined tribes, and he promised to make his people keep the peace and respect the Mexican authorities. The Indians were to fight the enemies of Mexico and especially to prevent incursions of the Komanche, Lipan, and other raiding tribes. They were to deliver all loot captured to the nearest authorities. They were given some tools with which to build a village, and a small daily food subsidy. According to this treaty, Wild Cat and all tribes with him were to renounce all salaries or subsidies from the United States as they were considered Mexican citizens from that moment on, with all rights and privileges.

The second, and more permanent migration of Kickapoo to Mexico took place in 1862 when a band of about 250, wishing to avoid involvement in the Civil War, and incensed by the Treaty of 1862 opening their country to a railroad, moved into northern Coahuila. In October, 1864, they appeared before the alcalde of Santa Rosa to ask permission to remain in that municipality until they could obtain a permanent place of residence from the president of the Republic (Mexican Committee of Investigation, p. 411). Permission was obtained, and in 1866 a municipality act formally granted them the lands at Nacimiento left vacant by the Seminole, and this has been their home ever since. After the expulsion of the French from Mexico, President Benito Juarez in 1857 confirmed the grant of the municipality. In 1919 the Kickapoo gained permanent possession of their lands by decree of President Carranza, at which time they were assigned over 7,000 hectares of land.*

*Robert E. Ritzenthaler and Frederick A. Peterson, *The Mexican Kickapoo Indians*, pp. 17-20. Used by permission.

17

A KICKAPOO BIBLE

The Scriptures have never been translated into the Kickapoo language. They have never had missionaries, in the real sense of the word, until recently.

During the period just following the War of 1812, Isaac McCoy, a Baptist missionary, was laboring in southern Michigan and the northern parts of Indiana and Illinois. At that time a band of the Kickapoo were living in the vicinity of what is now Peoria, and it is possible that McCoy's work extended to that area.

McCoy's greatest problem was that the Indians were moving west faster than work could be established effectively among them. Funds from his headquarters were never sufficient to support his work as these were needed "to support a young missionary couple in Burma by the name of Judson."

McCoy finally gave up the struggle and teamed up with the government forces that were engaged in moving the Indians to the west of the Mississippi. His objective in this, quite in contrast to that of the government, was to see the Indians removed from the baleful influences of the white traders and settlers.

In 1818 we find McCoy in Iowa and in contact with a band of the Kickapoos. They must have been in transit at the time, as we find in the record no permanent settlement of Kickapoos in Iowa. McCoy writes to his board as follows:

> It will afford pleasure to the board to know, that since my last [report] the situation of the Wea and Kickapoo Indians has attracted my attention materially. They have heard the proposal of the Kentucky Missionary Society, "to take some of the children instituted for that purpose." These proposals were made to the Weas through their agent. After several weeks deliberation on the subject, they returned for answer that "they were unwilling to send their children to Kentucky to be educated, because that, in obtaining an English education, they would lose their mother tongue, and if they had learned anything profitable, they would be unable to communicate it to their friends at home; but if schools could be established in their neighborhood, where the children could get an English education, it would be agreeable to their wishes."*

Nothing came of McCoy's attempts to educate members of the tribe, and this band must have joined the bands in Illinois where they remained until the 1830s.

During the turbulent years of Indian removal, first from east of the Mississippi and then to Indian territory, missionary effort was never developed. During this period too, the management of the Indians was transferred to

*"Letter from Isaac McCoy, Jan. 14, 1818," in *The Latter Day Luminary* (Philadelphia: Bapt. Brd. of For. Missions for the US, 1818).

the War Department, and it was not until the administration of U. S. Grant that the idea was proposed to have "religious persons" serve as the Indian agents, and missionaries appointed to undertake the "education, civilization and Christianization" of the Indians.

By the time Grant's "peace policy" was in force, the Kickapoos were divided into three bands, one in northeastern Kansas, one in Oklahoma and a third, the largest group, in Coahuila State in Mexico, where they had fled to escape involvement in the Civil War.

The annual report to the Department of the Interior for 1901 reveals that no missionary had been appointed to the reservation in Kansas. A missionary from the Quakers was appointed to the band in Oklahoma, but his duties were to educate and teach the Indians to farm (they had been successful farmers in Illinois for many years).

They numbered 426 in 1875 and were allotted "160 acres of the best land in the area." The mission property took ten acres of this allotment. This means that the concentration of population on this particular quarter section was 1704 per square mile, which is three times as dense as it was in New Jersey in 1970, which is the most densely populated state in the union. The land allowance would figure about 1.5 acres per family. The Kickapoos were expected to become farmers.

The 1901 report of the Indian agent to the Department of the Interior reads as follows:

> It is usual for considerable stress to be placed on the religious work among the Indians. My close observation has been that those engaged in missionary

> work are only sympathizers; . . . They have toiled among the Kickapoos for the past 25 years. The government has set aside 160 acres of the most desirable land in this country for their use and purpose. The Society of Friends has improved this tract and through their missionaries occupy it as a mission school, and while a considerable amount of money has been spent for the support of those missionaries they do not accomplish that which they might for the Indians because of their ever persistent efforts to force their religious views on the Indians always ignoring the fact that the Kickapoo is as thoroughly imbued with and has as distinct a conception of the Creator as they have; that he lives as religious a life as they do; that he in his way is as prayerful as they are. He blesses his food by inviting the attention of the Great Spirit before whom he humbles himself and returns thanks for having received past blessings and asks their continuence.†

The Indian agent was correct in his estimate of the morality and piety of the Kickapoos. They were, as far back as records are available, devout theists who, however, had not heard the truth of the coming of the Saviour.

If the missionaries taught, as most missionaries did, that the god of the Indians was a pagan god while theirs was the true God, they were sadly deficient in any representation of Christian teaching that they may have made. Certainly the tribe did not become a Christian tribe under their ministrations.

†*Annual Report to the Department of the Interior, 1901* (Washington, D.C.: Government Printing Office, 1901), p. 339.

Indian missionaries of the Indian Gospel Crusade came to the Oklahoma band in the 1960s with splendid results. This is the band from which Walter Kaskuske came.

The Mexican Kickapoos in Coahuila State had no missionaries but continued in their old tribal belief in the Most High, with a ritualism that included a number of superstitions that are about as sinister as our walking under a ladder, avoiding black cats, and cherishing rabbit's feet.

On graduation Walter Kaskuske, under the auspices of the Indian Gospel Crusade, went as a missionary to the Mexican band.

At this time, Wycliffe Translators are on the field at Muzquiz, Coahuila, and are making good progress in reducing the ancient language to writing. Thus the day is breaking for the Kickapoos.

18

HUALAPAI

Stop at the Qumacho restaurant as you pass through Peach Springs, Arizona. You will be served by courteous, charming Hualapai waitresses with meals prepared by buxom Hualapai mothers. You will be served beefsteaks from the native cattle herd.

You are in the agency town of the Hualapai tribe. You will want to drop into the native craft store and visit with the friendly folks.

It is dry-looking country, but it is big, and that is the way the Hualapai like it. If the vegetation seems sparse, don't worry. The country has plenty of pasture for the cattle and horses and stretches away to the skyline to the north, where the country breaks down into the Grand Canyon of the Colorado.

The Hualapai have had low points in their existence. They were pretty well beaten down toward the last years of the last century. They are coming up again and are at the high point of their population growth. They are a small tribe, not more than eight hundred.

Missionaries Jim and Lillian Anderson came to the

tribe in 1916, and today there is still a strong element of evangelical Christianity in the tribe. Like most tribes they have taken may of the culture items of the surrounding whites, but they are still quite Indian in their thinking and speech. One still hears, after an exposure to white influences of over one hundred years, the children arguing with each other in the old native language. This demonstrates that the language in the home is still the Hualapai.

19

BILL IMUS

A rampaging Brahma bull put Bill Imus in the hospital. Gored and trampled, Bill obviously would never again perform in the rodeo circuit.

It may seem a bit extreme to say that this is the only way God could get Bill's attention. God had more profitable exploits for him.

As a small boy, on the Hualapai reservation in western Arizona, Bill sat in the released-time classes of the very practical missionaries, Jim and Lillian Anderson. The Andersons believed in having their little Indians memorize key passages of Scripture. Bill memorized John 3:16 and a lot of other verses, even if he did not pay much attention to what they meant at that time. He remembered the verses thirty years later when he needed their message.

By all rules of the game, the Hualapai should have been eliminated long ago or absorbed into the white man's world. This probably would have happened if it had not been for the influence of such persons as the

Andersons and a few concerned school teachers, nurses, and government agency people.

It is the history of the small Indian tribes (the Hualapai numbered 400 in 1920) that, when they are on the routes traveled by the dominating white culture, they disintegrate as tribes. The Hualapai were in such a plight. The only logical route of traffic from the Spanish settlements in New Mexico to the Colorado River and the California settlements, was along the relatively flat country south of the Grand Canyon. The last two hundred miles before the exploring trains reached the Colorado was the ancestral home of the Hualapai and their cousin tribe, the Yavapai.

The first white man to encounter the Hualapai was Padre Francisco Tomas Garces, who, with his exploring party of Spaniards, passed through northwestern Arizona in 1776 on an exploring journey starting at the delta of the Colorado and terminating in the Hopi mesas. He visited the Hummahabas (Mojaves) at what is now known as The Needles, and he descended into the canyon of the Havasupais and then went on to discover the Grand Canyon and be baffled by it. He visited the Hopi villages and then returned to the delta of the Colorado where he established the Purisima Mission.

His line of travel would have been along the water courses where the Hualapai had their villages. He may not have seen many of them, as they were nomadic hunters and gatherers, ranging from the desert to the forests along the south rim of the Grand Canyon. Garces attempted to do missionary work as he traveled and used as a visual aid a banner which showed a picture of the Virgin and Christ Child on one side and the flames of hell on the other. The Indians, of course, always chose the side that showed the Virgin.

The next whites to penetrate the country were the mountain men and trappers during the 1820s and 1830s. Such men as William Sherley (Old Bill) Williams, Paulino Weaver, and Jedediah Smith. These men trapped for beaver, prospected for gold, and acted as guides for military men or exploring parties that may have required their services.

Old Bill left his name in the area with a rather negligible range of mountains named for him and the city of Williams. Old Bill was something of a lone wolf whose reputation was questionable. It was said to be unlucky to walk ahead of Bill on the trail. Bill had the reputation of having resorted to cannibalism when necessary.

Jedediah Smith, another mountain man, was said to have carried a Bible with him in his travels. How well he used it is not stated. He passed through Hualapai country in 1826. His trail crossed the Colorado River at a point near where Hoover Dam is now located and continued south to The Needles, where he crossed again into California. While he got along with the Indians as a rule, somehow he antagonized the Mohaves in southern Nevada and narrowly escaped death.

Paulino Weaver must have entered Hualapai country, because we find that he married a Chemehuevi squaw. This tribe lives to the west and north of the Hualapai, and Weaver came from the southeast.

While these mountain men and trappers usually got along well with the Indians, they certainly were not famous for their morals, and the Indians always came off second best in any dealings with them.

The next and probably the most upsetting experience of the tribe was the coming of the military expeditions in connection with the Mexican War. The entire area was part of Mexico and would, during the years 1846 to 1848, be conquered and occupied by the United States military. Mexicans and Americans were equally ruthless when it came to warfare.

In 1846 and 1847 General Kearney's army and the Mormon battalion, blazing trails for the wagon roads that would follow, passed safely to the south of the Hualapai along the Gila River, but scouting parties probed in all directions for passable routes and, of course, found the route along the northern part of the area from Fort Defiance to The Needles.

Indians were always in danger. If Indians in one area resisted the scouting parties and killed the whites, the next Indians in the route of march would pay the penalty. The only safety for the Indians was to hide.

With the Treaty of Guadalupe Hidalgo signed in 1848, the whole area north of the present Mexican line was in possession of the Americans. New roads were opened along latitude 35. The gold rush of 1849 in California increased the westward flow of whites. Between 1853 and 1857, five road-building surveys went through the Hualapai country.

The excitement was greatest with the coming of Lieutenant Edward F. Beale and his caravan of freight-carrying camels. The camel caravans were the brainchild of Jefferson Davis, secretary of war at the time. The camels fared well enough and did a splendid job of transportation through the waterless desert, but the American teamsters did not know how to handle them. The project was abandoned. Some of the camels were acquired by individual owners, but many of them were turned loose in the desert, where they survived for many years. Sightings of lone camels were still being told into the present century.

Intrusions by the white forces increased in numbers and violence following the Civil War. Railroads were planned, and, in the 1880s, the Atlantic and Pacific, now the Santa Fe, went right through the Hualapai villages following the principal road. The railroads brought tourists, and the tourists eventually demanded better automobile roads. The gravel road through the Hualapai country was paved and then improved to become Highway 66 and is now Interstate 40.

The missionaries, Jim and Lillian Anderson, came in 1916; and their home is still to be seen from the freeway at the little village of Valentine.

And yet the Hualapai survived and remained Hualapai. They adopted what they chose of the white man's cultural offerings. They learned English but retained their tribal language. Hualapai youngsters still chatter with each other on the schoolyard in their own speech, which indicates that the native language is still the language of the home. They have retained some of their old handcraft skills, although in the tribal store the wares of a number of other tribes are offered, such as Navajo rugs and Papago baskets.

They have not intermarried with the whites. When

suitable mates are not available in the tribe, they will take mates from the surrounding tribes, the Mohave, the Havasupai, and even the Paiutes of Nevada.

They have developed a sizeable cattle herd, have some fine timber on the south rim of the Grand Canyon, and take good advantage of the tourist trade. Their men are in demand as herders.

Like most tribes that survived the low years of Indian population and morale, the Hualapai have doubled in number since the 1920s.

The preserving factor of the tribe was the influence of such persons as the Andersons and a more than usual number of Christian school teachers and government agents. The Andersons served the tribe as missionaries and counsellors for over fifty years. After Jim died, Lillian remained with her chosen friends until well into her eighties. It was common to see her at age eighty driving through the reservation in her Ford pickup or lined up with the other Indians at a tribal potluck. They gave her the most honorific title that it was possible to give, but which comes out in English as a rather drab title, "The Old Woman." Actually this was according her the position of tribal matriarch.

The tribal council has a majority of members who are active Christians. The native church is led by lay members of the tribe, with a larger than usual attendance by tribal members.

Bill Imus, in the process of recovering from his episode with the Brahma bull, recalled the verses of Scripture memorized as a boy, and with the counselling by the missionary and concerned Christian members of the tribe, applied the great transforming truth of John 3:16 and a totally new life ensued. The "new creature" called for nourishment, and Bill spent much time in the Word of God. Friends suggested Bible institute training.

Bill, a graduate of Haskell Indian School in Kansas, was academically qualified to take such schoolwork, and so, with his wife, Jenny, he enrolled, a middle-aged person with little background that would fit him for Bible school, except a desire to learn all about a subject that he had ignored for half a lifetime.

Indian people invariably bring to the classrooms a different and sometimes startling language. Unfortunately we English-speaking whites, with a long-standing background of Christian culture, affect a pious manner of speech and a theological language that is quite foreign to those of such a culture as middle-aged American Indians, whose daily contact with users of white man's English is on the street, in the business office, and—in Bill's case—the rodeo circuit.

We are sometimes rather shaken by the jargon in which these practical Christians express deep theological thoughts and the experiences of the Christian life. We are delighted, however, when we find that they are far better able to communicate their message to their own people than we, who have spent a lifetime trying to be exact in our theological expression.

I have been startled to hear my messages relayed in a simpler form of English, or in desperation, a native coworker will translate the message into the native because the listeners can't understand the speaker's English.

If one is aware of the structure of the native language,

he will notice "Indianisms" creeping into the English speech of the native. There will be native grammatical forms expressed in English words that have been groped after by the native speaker.

This whole process emphasizes the need for indigenous methods and has a tendency to make the white missionary a humbler person.

Bill's exhortations and expositions contained the jargon of the rodeo circuit, and his illustrations were quite understandable to his native auditors. His use of such expressions made one to realize that God is more interested in the heart's desire of His suppliants than He is in the language used to express them.

On one occasion Bill was praying in chapel. He was pondering over this new experience of having fellowship with Christian men of other Indian tribes. He was pondering too the fact that such a small number of Christian Indians had so many non-Christians to reach with the Gospel. With tears coursing down his cheeks, he prayed, "Lord, make us real Christians, not these whitewashed kind. Make us the real McCoy." The Lord understood Bill's figure of speech.

Recovered from his accident and now equipped with a working knowledge of the Word of God, he went back to the reservation to serve the Lord as well as carry his weight in the work of the tribe. He was made manager of the tribal cattle herd. But that wasn't all. Bill was destined to become a missionary.

The Sobobas, one of the so-called mission tribes of California, would have nothing to do with the white man's religion. They had lived for centuries in a beautiful, small canyon at the foot of the San Jacinto mountains. A beautiful perenniel spring coursed through their canyon, which was lined with a variety of verdure including the stately Washingtonia palms and live oak. Hot springs emerged from the rocks at the mouth of the canyon.

This oasis was too attractive to be wasted on unappreciative aborigines, and, in due time, by the usual means of pushing and persuading, the Indians were relocated on a sandy bench of chaparrel and desert about two miles from their ancestral canyon.

The cottages of affluent whites now line the banks of the canyon. The hot springs are now a health resort where visitors soak away their "humors" in the healing waters.

The Sobobas live within a few miles of two small cities in what is known as the old Spanish California. At least a half-dozen evangelical churches flourish in the area. A number of times, the concerned members of these churches had attempted to reach the Indians but with no success. The Indian response was always the same: "You took our land. We don't want your religion." It would take an Indian to reach these Indians.

Bill Imus volunteered. An old jalopy that would not attract attention was provided, and Bill was sent in, without introduction by any white man, to do what he could. Very humiliating to the white man indeed!

He waved cheerily to the padre whose house commanded the entrance to the village and went unchallenged on his way. A Soboba, with the hood of his car raised, was tinkering with his motor. Bill looked in the other side and said hello. The Soboba looked up, and exclaimed, "Hey, aren't you Bill Imus?" Sure enough, he and Bill had attended Haskell Institute in Kansas together. Bill's first hurdle was over, and he was satisfactorily introduced.

The two old friends exchanged information on what each had been doing for the past years, and Bill had a splendid opportunity to tell Charley Sanchez about his new attachment to Jesus Christ and deluged Charley with an impromptu sermon in the language of the rodeo circuit, which Charley understood. This wasn't the white man's religion: it had always sounded different. Bill told him that it was so good that he wanted to tell all the Sobobas about it.

Charley and the tribe responded in true Indian fashion. They had a potluck and a full scale picnic, with Bill as guest of honor. Not only did Bill have opportunity to visit all of the families in their homes but to speak to all of them in a public meeting in the tribal headquarters.

Bill went back and forth between his job with the tribal herd on the Hualapai reservation and his mission field on the Soboba reservation. He accomplished in a few months what had not been possible in a hundred years by white missionaries.

Bill's ministry was shortened. We read with sorrow in the newspaper: "Bill Imus, Hualapai Indian from Peach Springs, Arizona, killed in a two car crash on Highway 66." But Bill had fulfilled his part in the Great Commission: he had carried the message, effectively, to his part of the world.

20

LEO POWSKY'S JAIL MINISTRY

Leo and Rita Powsky were led to the Lord by Bill Imus.* Bill and Leo were cousins.

Under the teaching of Lillian Anderson, Leo and Rita had memorized the same portions of Scripture as Bill. At the time of crisis in Leo's life, the words of John 3:16 came back to him.

All of the Hualapai and Havasupai knew Leo, and when he would encounter them on the street or in the jail at Flagstaff during his Bible school days, something was bound to happen.

One day in class, Leo asked, "What is this 'glory' word in the Bible?" Webster's definition or, in fact, the definition of any theologian would have been lost on Leo.

The teacher was perplexed, and then he recalled an incident from the jail ministry. He said, "Remember, Leo, that time in the jail house when you were talking to

*Their story is told in the author's book, *No Dark Valley*.

your cousin who was in the cell? You had been reading your Bible to him and explaining salvation, and you were both weeping? That was glory."

The Hualapai Tribe had just finished a new jail on the reservation when Leo went back to serve as vice-chairman of the tribal council. Leo went promptly to work with the jail house as his parish. "Too bad we built the new jail; after a while we aren't going to need it!" he said once.

Some months later, I met Leo in the agency town of Peach Springs. Leo reported, "I got the jail nearly empty—all getting saved—down to one man right now. We'll get him soon!"

21

MISSIONARY WORK AMONG THE YUMA TRIBES

There has never been a concentrated effort to reach the river tribes. The tribes of the southwest were visited by the Spanish Jesuit, Eusebio Kino, in the seventeenth century, but little notice is given of any work among the tribes at the delta. He was very vigorous in promoting the Roman rituals among the Pima and Papago. Several missions were established, but the remaining buildings are most important as tourist attractions.

The Diegueno and Juaneno tribes were encountered by the Franciscans under Junipero Serra and became units of what have been called the Mission Indians. This fatal episode in attempted missionization and acculturation ended with the Mexican Revolution of the 1820s, and by this time the Mission Indians had become so depleted that their tribal entity was never again realized, and the few who escaped returned to their own homes where it was possible.

Padre Francisco Tomas Garces, entering the area in

1768, reported that Kino's work was completely abandoned, with no traces of Christian knowledge remaining.

Garces built the Purisimo mission near what is now Yuma, but across the river in California. Unfortunately the gentle padre and the arrogant Spanish military were at such cross purposes in dealing with the Indians, that the Indians arose in indignation and destroyed both the military and Father Garces.

With the establishment of the reservation system by the U. S. government, the Yuma tribe was assigned to the Episcopalian Church. Nothing seems to have been accomplished, as the Yumas were utterly disinterested in ritualistic religion or even in their old religious system.

The Maricopas, who joined forces with the Papago, have been touched in recent years (along with the Papagos) by the Mission to the Migrants. Students studying at Arizona Bible Institute, later Arizona Bible College, also had some success in reaching them.

The Mohaves have had some Christian teaching, largely because they have lived in and around the town of The Needles. A number of Christians are among them. Nazarenes have done effective work among them.

The Hualapai were the most fortunate of the river tribes to have missionaries Jim and Lillian Anderson for more than half a century. The Andersons also labored with the Havasupai living in their Cataract Canyon.

The Indian agent responsible for both tribes who lived at thc Hualapai agency was cooperative in seeing that opportunities to present the Gospel were available.

The Havasupai tribe, in Cataract Canyon, was fortunate in having, for seven years, the services of a devoted

Christian government nurse, Florence Barker. Florence was missionary as well as nurse during those years and was well loved by these people of the bluegreen water.

The Episcopal Church built a chapel on the floor of the canyon in the 1950s. It was necessary to fly the parts of the building in by helicopter. A resident missionary lived in the canyon for a time, but the tribal response was negative. The chapel was given to the United Indian Mission. Missionaries John and Rie Greenwood took over the work.

Several members of the tribe, as well as of the Hualapai, attended Southwestern School of Missions in Flagstaff.

22

APACHE

"I was there in that solitary cell, just a cold concrete floor, no blanket, nothing. There was a hole in the door where food was brought to me."

Here was a young Apache, born to roam as freely as any wild thing, caught in the stinking trap designed by the white man for the correction of the "hostiles" who dared to defy the authority of their conquerors. But this was now an Apache jail, and Allan was there because he was a bad Apache.

Allan was born and grew to young manhood on the San Carlos Apache Reservation. As a boy he would go with his family each Sunday to a place the Apaches considered sacred. All morning the members of the tribe would sing and chant. They would then go and sing over sick ones at the direction of the medicine man.

The Apaches had accumulated a strange mixture of religious rites. Being nomads, they had medicine men or shamans who chanted and charmed away the sicknesses and evil spirits. Their rites were similar to those of the Navajos; the Apache and Navajo are cousin tribes. During the three hundred years of contact with the Spaniards, they had picked up a number of half pagan, half Christian ideas. In their devil dance, for instance, there is the presence of the cruciform. There were no missionaries to the Apaches, either Catholic or Protestant, until the present century.

Until that morning in the San Carlos jail, Allan had never heard a word of the Gospel of salvation and, as far as he remembers, had never seen a Bible.

An Indian, a Pima named Don Rovie, was preaching to the inmates of the jail. Allan was in solitary, but he was listening to what this Pima was telling of how he too was freed from his sins in a jail house in Los Angeles, where he was facing trial for armed robbery.

Allan wanted to hear more and petitioned the authorities to permit Don to visit him in the jail house. This was granted. Allan tells of the interview: "I was sitting there thinking about my life. How cruel I had been against my mother and family. I listened to Mr. Rovie as he told how his life had been so much like mine. He told how he had accepted Christ in a Los Angeles jail cell while awaiting trial. When he realized that Jesus died for him on calvary's cross, he trusted in Him as Saviour, and Christ changed his life. As I listened the Spirit of God showed me it was Jesus alone that had the power to change my life. I got on my knees in that dark cell and prayed, confessing my sins and trusting in Christ as Saviour and Lord. I had a wonderful experience with the Lord that I cannot put into words."

The wild thing was tamed but was still in the cage. The jailer noticed the change. The new creature was beginning to show through. The jailer told the judge, and they both watched for the next two weeks. Was Allan putting on a front? Had he just "got religion"? The jailer thought it was real. He was a Christian and knew the signs of the new life.

They were most anxious to be rid of their problem prisoner and decided that they could parole him. They came to him with a proposition. The judge said, "Allan, if this is real, we are going to release you. Tonight we are going to take off your handcuffs and leave the cell door unlocked. If you are still here in the morning we are going to let you go." Allan was there.

Allan was out in the sunlight in more ways than one. He attended some revival meetings being held by Don and then Bible school was proposed.

Oh yes, there was a wedding. Allan had been involved with sixteen-year-old Valencia, and the judge required that they get married before coming to Flagstaff to school.

It was the beginning of the winter semester, and Allan and Valencia were enrolled in my class in the doctrine of the new birth. Here was this young couple, newly emerged from an environment of viciousness; what could they absorb? They had no Christian background or training. They had known no Christians and knew nothing of the language of Christianity. But, for two weeks now, they had been in possession of a fragment of knowledge that, somehow, by the magic of a name—Jesus—they had been transported into a new world.

The years of running away were ended. These newborn Apaches were learning to sing hymns and study a new Book, the Bible, in company with other Indians—Navajos, Hopis, Sioux—many of whom had been renegades like themselves. It was a whole new world, and Allan and Valencia liked it, even if they did not understand it.

The dean was having mixed thoughts. Was the doctrine of the new birth just theological subject matter, or was it functional? What could he expect of these two who could not even have expressed in words what had happened a few days before when they had "trusted Jesus."

The Scriptures had said plainly enough that "if any man be in Christ he is a new creature"; here was an opportunity to see the new creature emerge in these previously sin-ridden and sin-scarred candidates for transformation.

Practical problems started to develop. Allan and Valencia had thirty-five cents between them when they arrived at school. Soon there was a new baby girl to take care of. Some sort of a home must be established.

Allan got a job on the custodial staff at the Northern Arizona University. His work was so satisfactory that he was soon assigned full charge of the science building where his assistants called him "Chief." Regular wages were a new thing for Allan, and any amount, regularly, was better than the intermittent poverty and quick riches of the old life.

A problem, related to the old days, was bothering Allan. He asked permission to go back to the reservation where he had some business to take care of. He assured us that he would not get himself into any trouble. A few days later he returned with two little Apache boys in tow.

He explained, "These are my sons from the old wild oats days. Now that I am a Christian, I must make a Christian home for my boys."

23

HOSTILES AND FRIENDLIES

The Apaches have survived in the pulp magazines and the TV thrillers as the "bad guys" in the history of the Southwest. Today one's scalp is perfectly safe on the streets of Phoenix or Tucson, as far as Apaches are concerned, but one still encounters old-timers who wax quite wrathful as they tell about their "grandpappy" who was scalped by a miserable " 'Pache savage."

Away back in 1540 when the peaceful Pueblos submitted to Francisco Vasquez de Coronado and his army of priests, horsemen, and Mexican neophytes, it was only the nomadic Apaches who put up a fight in defense of their desert country. Three centuries later, when the *Americanos* began to crisscross the territory with their traders, cavalry, and railroad surveyors, it was the Apaches who put up the final fight for their country, and lost.

All of the Pueblo people, except for the Acomas (who were virtually exterminated for their resistance), kissed the crucifix and allowed the priests to build chapels and baptize their youngsters with Spanish names, such as Pedro, Pablo, and Jose.

Both priests and Indians made concessions so that the church feast days would coincide with the native calendar of pagan festivals and seasonal rituals. Thus the Catholic feast of Easter was made to coincide with the festival of the sun goddess. The black basalt figurine of the sun goddess had been rechristened as "The Black Virgin of Guadaloupe."

On the feast days the Pueblo Indians still troop to the padre's chapel to hear mass. They then parade the effigy of their local patron saint, Maria, Jose, or Tomas, and place it on a pedestal in the plaza and proceed with their own pagan dance. Thus the local padre and the tribal priests are both satisfied. They are pagans with crucifixes.

The Apaches, to the utter frustration of the Spanish troops, could not be pinned down. They had no permanent villages, were not settled farmers like the Pueblos, and had no single tribal head with whom the Spaniards could make treaties. They were hunters and gatherers of wild foods ranging over millions of acres of semidesert valleys and mountains. Unlike their tribal cousins, the Navajos, they did not adopt sheepherding. They did acquire horses from the Spaniards, however, which increased their capacity to roam.

The Apaches loved their freedom in the wild mountainous country on both sides of the Mexican border. This they considered their rightful homeland, and they defended it fiercely for three hundred years, from the time of Coronado until their final defeat and captivity in the last decade of the nineteenth century.

The vigorous defense of their homeland brought them

the appellation of "hostiles," whereas the sedentary Pueblos in New Mexico and the farming Pimas in Arizona were listed as "friendlies." Mangas Coloradas, Shatto, Cochise, and Geronimo, the prominent characters of the TV Westerns, are the epitome of Apache resistance to the white man's attempts to control and civilize.

Allan Earley, the Apache of the previous chapter, was cast in the mold of old Geronimo. He resented the restraints of civilization and hated the white man. Put him in braids, headband, and deerskin leggings, and he would be quite recognizable as kin to the old warrior.

Like all Apache boys, he had grown up in the company of the men and boys of the clan. Allan chafed under the restraint when he was forced to attend school. He much preferred the native instruction, administered by his uncles, in the lore of the tribe, the life ways of the Apache, the skills of hunting and trapping. He would break away from the school life and return to the tribe only to be captured and brought back. This became a way of life for the restless native boy.

There had been no open warfare or raiding for over fifty years before Allan was born on the San Carlos reservation, but many of the old ones, including descendents of Cochise and Geronimo, remembered the final days of the Apache wars, the forced marches to inadequate reservations, the starvation, the attempts to exterminate the tribe, and finally the surrender (they never did catch him) of Geronimo and his little band of holdouts. They remembered the old warrior in handcuffs on his way to imprisonment in Florida in violation of the amnesty that had been promised. They remembered the bounty hunters who got rich on Apache scalps which were easier to obtain than beaver pelts.

In the 1830s, the governors of Sonora and Chihuahua offered bounties for the Apache scalps. The prices offered were one hundred dollars for male scalps, fifty for female and twenty-five for children's scalps.

James Kirker, a trapper and mountain man, organized a company of two hundred to engage in scalp hunting, and the results were so great that the Mexican officials demurred in paying such amounts. Kirker's best year was 1839, when he made $100,000.*

Allan, of course, absorbed all of this hatred from boyhood, and after he went to school, he particularly resented the emphasis of history, the glamorous deeds and bravery of the white soldiers and settlers and the abominable deeds of the savage Apache killers. There is still much of this in the textbooks of the Southwest.

School attendance was bondage, and his truancies were frequent but always ended in a forcible return to the hated schoolroom. In spite of this, he acquired a good working knowledge of English.

A pattern of life emerged. The petty thefts of his truancies grew to be robberies as he grew older. The fist fights grew into muggings and robbery. He became a regular inmate of the tribal jail.

He developed a skill at jail-breaking and continued his "breaking and entering," now with a girl accomplice, a fifteen-year-old delinquent. Apprehended, he was

*Madeline Pare, *Arizona Pageant* (Phoenix: Arizona Historical Foundation, 1965), p. 77.

placed in solitary confinement in irons. He had come to the end of the trail in a situation not dissimilar to that of old Geronimo.

Where were the missionaries all of this time? The early Spaniards traveled with a crucifix in one hand and a sword in the other. If the crucifix was rejected the sword was invoked. They at least thought that they were being consistent. The Protestant Americans knew that you could not travel with a gun in one hand and a Bible in the other, so they discarded the Bible.

It is a notable fact that there were no missionaries to the Indians in the West until after the period of Indian removal, with the exception of the Whitman-Spalding party of missionaries to the Oregon country in the late 1830s. This missionary episode terminated in the Whitman massacre about ten years later.

Two military men with religious upbringing encountered the Indians. Col. John Chivington of the Colorado reservists had been a Methodist circuit rider but is better known as the commander of the military expedition that massacred the Cheyenne village at Sand Creek in 1859, indiscriminately killing men, women, and children in a predawn surprise raid in a camp that had been assured of government protection. Both the American flag and the flag of truce were violated in the massacre. Chivington was eventually unfrocked by the church and drummed out of the military.

Gen. O. O. Howard was one military leader who was universally respected as a Christian and known as the praying general. He always refused to fight on Sunday. While he was, to some degree, considerate of the Indians, he pursued his duty as a soldier but made little impression on the Indians as a sympathetic Christian.

Chapter 22 told how Allan found Christ and ended up at Southwestern School of Missions. The first semester was rather tough for Allan. He had had no knowledge of the Bible when he first sat down in the classroom. By the end of the first semester, there was definite progress and he could well explain the plan of salvation both from his textbooks and his personal experience.

As soon as school was dismissed, Allan went back to San Carlos and started making amends for the knavery of the old days. Now he was going around the village talking to the people he had mugged and robbed. He was demonstrating the power of the Gospel, and his folks could see his point.

Each vacation period saw him going back to witness to the folks at San Carlos. On several occasions during the school years, he took gospel teams of Indian students to the reservation. Apaches were hearing the same message as Allan was telling them from Kickapoos, Hopis, Navajos, and Sioux. Other Apaches started coming to school.

Allan's work in school continued to be top level. He got straight *A* grades from the second semester on. In his last semester, he was student-body president and was teaching in the classroom.

Allan discovered books. He was delighted when he became acquainted with the wealth of writings that were available to him in his study of the Word of God.

In addition to the school library, he discovered that there was a bookstore where he could buy books to start his own library. Allan would select a title from the shelves and study it for a while. When he decided that he wanted that particular volume, he would pay the attendant twenty-five cents. He would then stand and read for a considerable time and replace the book. Whenever he had free moments he would return and read and make a twenty-five cent payment. The book would be read by the time he had it paid for; then he would take it home.

By graduation time, Allan had a small but choice library of commentaries, biographies, and reference works, that would be a credit to any discerning pastor or Bible student.

Indians have long since discovered the eloquence of silence. Whites become restless if thirty seconds pass without something happening. A whole minute of silence is unendurable.

One can learn much from the manner in which Indians can enjoy quiet contemplation and silent fellowship with another of the same kind. After such an interlude of silent meditation, a single word can convey as much meaning as if a whole poem were written.

Graduation time had come for Allan. Coincidental with it, I was removed from the classroom scene. Allan was seen crossing the campus toward our house. What could he want?

He came in quietly and sat down on the davenport. He smiled and said nothing. For the first fifteen minutes, I said nothing and smiled. Then, just in case there was a problem, I asked, "Was there something you wished to see me about, Allan?"

"No," he said, "but I heard you were going away, and I might not see you for a while. I just wanted to have some fellowship." So we sat and smiled, and I thought I could follow his thoughts as we meditated. *The old life—the pagan dances—the fist fights—the blood—the drinking—the bad women—the stinking jail—the handcuffs—and now the great change—the scars of sin all gone—a happy family of five of us—groceries paid for—dear friends in school and on the reservations—singing with happy hearts—Apaches listening to the Gospel and weeping over their sins—and then smiling—a lifetime of work to do for Jesus—and the assurance of salvation in the heart.* How could you say all that in conversation? It just wouldn't come out in words.

And I sat and thought too. *Down the years with wonderful Indian people—listening to Grandma Ike, up on the Cowlitz, as she told of her experiences and her love for "Papa Jesus"—Old Silas Heck and his people sitting on logs around an evening fire on the Chehalis reservation—singing Silas' own song "I love Jesus, Hi Ho"—sitting in hogans and on trading-post steps—visiting Indian friends in the hospital and in the jail house—rolled up in a blanket all of a moonlit night in Monument Valley and seeing the sun's first beams lighting up the red sandstone buttes—turning the pages for Allan in the classroom—trying to help him get his old Buick started.*

It was a happy half hour of fellowship with not more than a dozen words exchanged. Allan went back to his studies, and I went back to packing books.

I had asked Allan, about the time of his graduation, what he planned to do when he was through school.

"First," he said, "I still have some making-right to do on the San Carlos reservation, and a lot of people down there to talk to about the Lord. Then I want to be a Bible-teaching evangelist, first in all the jails where there are Indians and then in the small tribes around the country where they have no missionaries."

Allan has done just that. I ran across his tracks in Minnesota. A friend who has worked with Indians for many years confided, "We are having our all-Indian Bible conference in a few weeks and we are having a Bible teacher from the West." "What tribe?" I asked. "Apache." "That could only mean Allan Earley." The missionary asked, "How did you know?" "Because there is only one Apache who knows his Bible well enough to teach at a conference."

A few weeks later, out of sheer curiosity, I wrote to my friend, "How did my boy do?" "Splendid" he replied. "It was the best conference we have had in twenty-five years."

Later adventures took Allan to the Paiutes in Nevada, the Penobscots in Maine, and a dozen others. Result? More young Indians are going to Bible school so that they can take the Gospel to their own people.

This is the indigenous principle in missions.

24

WHAT MADE GERONIMO FIGHT?

Small boys watching TV are all alert when old Geronimo is shown taking potshots at passing wagon trains. The old scoundrel is outwitted, however, by a company of the seventh cavalry, with guidons flying in the breeze. Old Geronimo slinks away with his band and is soon lost in the chapparal.

Undoubtedly, Geronimo was a savage killer. His whole recorded lifetime shows him raiding into Chihuahua and back again into Arizona. Also he was probably blamed for a lot of crimes that he did not commit. Someone had to be blamed.

Geronimo's experiences were among the last of a long series of clashes between the Apaches and the whites that started at the time of the conquest.

One of the reasons for the rapid conquest of the Pueblo tribes was that they hoped that the Spaniards would help protect them from the *Apachu de Nabahu* who were always making quick raids on the Pueblo corn patches. This was in 1540. At the time the Apaches must have been a rather small tribe, but they were persistent enough to be a nuisance to the village dwellers.

The Apaches finally became a nuisance on both sides of the border and were in constant skirmishes with the Spanish troops. Apparently the Apaches were quite successful, because we see them soon after in possession of Spanish horses and thus much more mobile in their raiding.

Stephen Longstreet tells of Geronimo's projection into a life time of marauding on both sides of the line.

> While he was raiding in Mexico, the tribe was massacred by Mexicans. Geronimo returned to find ninety women and children had been carried off and sold as slaves. His own mother, his wife and children had been brutally murdered. Only eight warriors were left. Nearly mad with grief, he hid his emotions. As he remembered that dreadful moment he said: "I did not pray nor did I decide to do anything in particular, for I had no purpose left, I finally followed the tribe silently." His nature became meaner.*

Geronimo lost no opportunity to avenge his family's murder. In fact, I suppose, he was trying to avenge all the slaughters of four hundred years of Apache-white clashes.

Madeline Pare relates a series of unfortunate clashes that perpetuated the hatred from decade to decade.

> James Johnson, a trapper and guide who was married to a Mexican, fractured any possible peace

*Stephen Longstreet, *War Cries on Horseback* (Garden City, N.Y.: Doubleday, 1970), pp. 93-94.

on the Arizona frontier in 1837 by an act of unparalleled treachery toward an Apache band. Johnson, because of his marriage, was allowed to pass freely through the lands of the Apache. Friendship developed between him and the Apache chieftain, Juan Jose, an able and fairly well educated man. . . .

Knowing of this friendship the governor of Sonora offered Johnson a large reward if he would bring about the death of Juan Jose. White savage that he was, Johnson agreed to perform the treacherous deed. He soon had his opportunity. An American party seeking to buy mules in Sonora had found the area stripped clean of them, due to Apache depredations. They wished to return north and Johnson persuaded them to go through Juan Jose's country, offering his services as a guide. The whole party went to the Apache camp near the Santa Rita Copper Mines where they received hospitality. . . .

Johnson handed out special treats he had brought for the Apache women and children. The Indians crowded around the sack of sweets. Then Johnson touched his cigar to a pack on one of the mules. A hidden blunderbuss loaded with balls, slugs and chains, was discharged into the group that was hovering over the sweets. Most of them were killed or wounded. One of Johnson's men who had taken Juan Jose aside for conversation, shot the chieftain at close range. As the Apache fell, he screamed to Johnson, "Save my life! I don't want to kill your friend." Johnson's treacherous reply was a lethal bullet.†

†Madeline Ferrin Pare and Bert M. Fireman, *Arizona Pageant,* pp. 75-76. Used by permission.

Scalping is usually attributed to the Indians as one of their barbarisms. Actually the Indians scalped rarely before their encounters with the whites. Scalping was taught to the Algonkians by the French, and the Iroquois learned it from the British who paid large bounties for Indian scalps. The system was used as a means of tallying the bounty payments.

The Apache learned it from the Spanish. Pare tells us of the system as it was used in the Spanish days.

> In the 1830's the governors of Sonora and Chihuahua entered into a particularly vile phase of Apache intimidation. They let contracts to white hunters whom they engaged to exterminate the Apaches. These men were to receive bounties in return for Apache scalps, both male and female, young and old. This desperate measure enlisted the services of ruthless, enterprising men such as Johnson. The prices paid were attractive, usually $100 for the scalp of a male, $50.00 for a female, and $25.00 for a child. This revolting activity proved to be lucrative. In fact, the scalp hunters at times brought back so many scalps that the authorities . . . demurred over payment.
>
> James Kirker, mountain man and adventurer . . . organized a company to engage in scalp hunting. He and his hunters brought back hundreds of scalps and claimed thousands of dollars in bounties. . . . Kirker's best year was in 1839, when he is reported to have made $100,000.‡

At the inception of the Civil War, the North and the South were in conflict over who should govern Arizona.

‡Pare and Fireman, p. 107.

The Confederates were just as bloody as the Northern troops, and John R. Baylor, Confederate, who was appointed governor of Arizona gave the following order.

> You will use all means to persuade the Apaches or any tribe to come in for the purpose of making peace, and when you get them together kill all the grown Indians and take the children prisoners, and sell them to defray the expense of killing the Indians. Buy whiskey and such other goods as may be necessary for the Indians and I will order vouchers given to cover the amount expended. Allow no Indians to escape.§

The Camp Grant Massacre was probably the most deliberate and one of the bloodiest. Camp Grant was located about seventy-five miles southeast of Tucson as a camp for the care and detention of Apache prisoners. The Indians were peaceful and gathered wild hay for the army horses and mules. The pay was small, but the Indians were quite busy with their job. The kindly treatment of the Indians riled the old Apache haters, and they decided to do something about it.

On April 28, 1870, a punitive expedition set out from Tucson for Camp Grant. The volunteer army included forty-eight Mexicans, six Americans, and ninety-four Papagos. They reached the post in the early morning. They used clubs and guns in the surprise attack and set the camp on fire. By the time the doctor got there, no medical aid was needed. Nearly all the dead were mutilated. Parc tells us the murderers returned to Tucson, bringing twenty-nine children to be kept as slaves. A

§Ibid.

trial was held at the demand of an outraged populace, but the local temper was so hostile that the participants were acquitted.||

Geronimo and his predecessors were nasty fighters and accounted for a lot of deaths of soldiers and pioneers, but they got their training from the whites. The whites had the guns so the Apaches lost the final fight.

||Pare and Fireman, pp. 122-23.

25

INDIANS OF THE NORTHWEST COAST

The Indian tribes living along the Northwest coast, from northern California to the Strait of Juan de Fuca, were among the last to be affected by the western march of the white population. In fact it is quite possible that small migrations from Asia were still arriving when the Europeans were "discovering" and exploring the East coast of America.

These Pacific Coast tribes were the richest of the Indians, living, as they did, in an area replete with fish and game for food, building materials for their homes, and waterways for their transportation. Weather was never as severe as it was inland and east of the mountains.

The Yuroks and Koroks in northern California built excellent houses of split redwood timbers and boards. The Chinooks and other Columbia River tribes had unbelievable runs of salmon of several varieties. The Quinaults and Quilautes along the coast of Washington built substantial lodges and also framed huge ocean-going canoes out of cedar logs. They were accomplished whalers. The Clallam women on the Olympic Peninsula were accomplished weavers and raised herds of small, white, wooly dogs, which were clipped for weaving.

The fifty or more tribes occupying the area were divided into ten language families, the largest of these being the Salish. It was my privilege to serve among a number of these Salish tribes including the Chehalis, Quinault, Queets, Skokomish, Nemah, Shoalwater, and Humptulips. The smaller of these tribes have now become absorbed into white culture areas or have moved to the reservations of other tribes. The larger tribes that remained on their reservations have doubled in population since the 1930s when I was working among them.

A few of the stories of these people belong in this collection.

26

NEMAH RIVER

The Nemah River flows through magnificent stands of virgin spruce and fir timber; at least, it did when I first traveled the gravel road that led along its banks. A logging railroad paralleled the roadway. The old-timers said that in the old days the salmon were so plentiful in the Nemah, "you could walk across the river on their backs." Cabins nestled in the clearings along the river, flanked by rank gardens of vegetables and flowers. It rains one hundred or more inches a year on the Nemah.

I banged on doors until my knuckles were sore without a response. I could see figures inside the houses, and there was smoke coming from the chimneys. I was ready to give up, when I came to the last cabin and knocked listlessly. Suddenly the door opened, and a cheerful looking old couple stood before me. He was a diminutive white man with a long white beard. He looked for all the world like a storybook gnome. Behind him stood the tallest, stateliest, and, I'm sure, the largest Indian woman I had ever seen. She loomed behind her husband like a backstop.

The old man was the soul of friendliness and courtesy. He laughed uproariously when I told him that no one else would come to the door. He didn't explain why. He had come from the gold diggings in California and found his squaw in this delightful wilderness and proceeded to sire a dozen stalwart sons. He had known something of Christianity in the old days and knew many of the old hymns; in fact, he "and the old lady used to sing them years ago." He was quite willing that the schoolhouse should be used for some meetings, so we arranged a date. He was the school board as well as the boss of the community. When I expressed my fears about the rest of the community with its unopened doors, he laughed again and said, "Don't worry, young fellow, at least me and my family will be there."

The old schoolhouse doubled as school and teacherage where the teacher lived with her grandfather. He was an old-fashioned Methodist who was delighted at the thought of "revival meetings."

It started to rain a few days before the meetings were to commence, and it rained steadily. Roads were flooded, and it was with considerable difficulty that I got through the high water to the schoolhouse. The teacher assured me that no one could get through the high water, but she suggested that the three of us could have a meeting anyway. Meeting time came and no audience. Then suddenly there developed sounds of racing motors, splashing water, and human voices, accompanied by headlights and swinging lanterns. It was the school bus being guided through the high water.

In the next five minutes, one hundred and three folks

of all sizes came into the schoolhouse and sat down, with the old man and his wife leading the procession. The old man chuckled, "This is my family!" These were the folks behind the closed doors who wouldn't do anything without the old man's say-so.

The room was so full that I was backed up to the chalk rail. I played and sang a couple of songs and then asked for favorites. "Shall We Gather at the River" seemed to be appropriate and so did "Sweet Hour of Prayer," but then the oldsters couldn't seem to remember any more. A youngster asked for "Strawberry Roan," and another asked for "Home on the Range," so I sang the versions that Howard Smith and I had arranged to these tunes for just such situations. After a few more songs out of my notebook, I prayed and read a chapter. Then an hour's sermon, an invitation, a closing hymn, and prayer. They sat.

The old man said, "Sing another song." I did. He said, "Sing another." I did. They still sat. Finally the old man said, "See here, young feller, when we go out for an evenin' to a doing we expect to stay all night." I sang another song, prayed, preached another sermon, gave another invitation, had a closing hymn and prayer. They seemed satisfied and then visited for another hour. It was then nearly midnight. They retraced their way through the high water, and the sound died in the dripping night.

I guess the moral to this story is, "Come, and bring your family!"

27

OYSTER TOWN

The old native-oyster aristocracy shuddered with horror at the thought of their staid little village becoming the very center of the crass, new Japanese oyster industry. But the native-oyster beds had played out, and the Johnny-come-latelys had discovered that the big, succulent Japanese oysters could make them a fortune, even in depression times. The tide flats of Shoalwater Bay were excellent oyster grounds, and there was cheap labor in the form of a whole tribe of local Indians ready to go to work in the packing plants. So the old, dignified native-oyster families sat in their two-story frame houses on the hill and sang their Episcopal hymns, while the newcomers sang and clapped to Pentecostal rhythms.

The old church was quite dilapidated, but the pews were still in place, and the pulpit looked like it would stand a little more pounding. On rainy days, the water funneled through the porch under the bell tower, but the steep roof over the main building shed the rain quite well. The old organ had long since become the home of a dozen families of mice and was unplayable. Billy Mink, a Salish Indian, the local guitarist, provided the music.

A friendly resident "allowed as how the town could stand some religion," and invited the missionary in to talk about the subject over the supper table. The fast-growing Japanese oysters sometimes were washed off the beds during a storm and deposited along the shore line. These were anybody's property and were a bonanza during those depression days. There was a saying current along the bay that "when the tide is out the table is spread." I had never eaten an oyster and had always held a deep admiration for the first primitive who decided to try one—long before the invention of Worcestershire sauce. Either he was very hungry or very curious. We had oysters for supper.

By bedtime my host decided that it was about time to find a bed for the missionary. It was obvious that his cabin was already too well occupied. We sallied out in the apparently deserted street, and a figure "hove to" out of the fog. It turned out to be Ben Swan, a half-breed who apparently thought it would be quite novel to have a preacher in his house.

Ben led in his car via a totally unimproved road through the brush and finally over a trestle made with parallel planks just the width of the tread of the car. We traveled over great distances of tidal slough and finally came to solid land and Ben's cabin, which seemed no larger than the one I had just left. It turned out to be a little more commodious, although as completely inhabited. There was one main room with a boxed-off cubicle in one corner and a ladder up the side of the cubicle. Other cubbyholes were discernible along another wall.

We made friends with the small fry by playing the guitar and singing. They turned out to be both children and grandchildren of Ben and his wife. Ben's wife showed unmistakable signs of being of Indian blood.

Ben was quite intrigued at the thought of having a preacher in his home for the first time. He was a little disappointed, however; he said, "You don't look like a preacher; you look more like a blankety-blank salesman." I didn't ask what he thought a preacher should look like.

I was finally ushered into the cubicle in the corner of the room while the family went through the ritual of preparing for the night by scrambling onto the platform over my room and disappearing into the various compartments along the west wall. The babel of retiring noises finally gave way to whispers and childish chuckles and then peace and quiet.

At four o'clock an old boiler of a jalopy ground across the trestle and came to a halt near the door. The car door slammed, and the front door rattled open, whereupon Ben hollered, "Hey, Rosie! There's a preacher in your bed!"

Rosie, who turned out to be the mother of several of the young fry, bellowed back, "What's a preacher doing in my bed?" Rosie was just returning from a Saturday night dance in the next town.

Between Rosie's homecoming and the rooster, I didn't get much sleep, but morning finally came, and breakfast—oysters! In fact it was oysters at every meal all week, until I came in my visiting to the homes of the old native-oyster aristocracy. They wouldn't deign to eat such common fare as Japanese oysters, so I had a few good "high church" meals.

Ben Swan's cabin turned out to be just a hundred yards from the beach at Shoalwater Bay, so as soon as possible that Sunday morning, I took my pocket Testament and found shelter on the lee side of a huge spruce drift log. I hadn't been there long when I became aware that I was not alone. Two of the little Swans had seen me go and followed. They insisted that I tell them some more of the stories I had told them the night before. They cuddled up beside me by the big log and listened with delight to the stories of the gospels.

There was no problem in getting a crowd at the old church. Any stranger in town is immediately spotted, and they all rather expected to hear the old bell ring. They came in twos and threes and families, a most heterogeneous audience of whites and Indians, Japanese and Chinese, Pentecostals and Papists, and sun worshipers, and they came every night all week. Some were saved, and a Sunday school was started.

On the last night the folks decided that the preacher should have something for his effort, and so, in the morning, they brought their offering—two sacks of oysters in the shell!

Not a very spectacular story—no plot—but as I visited there a year ago, thirty years later, I found that Billy Mink had long since gone to exchange his guitar for a harp and that the two little Swans, who first heard the gospel story behind the big log, are now leaders in the only evangelical church in the nearby town.

28

INDIAN SHAKERS

Some time in 1881, no one knows the exact date, John Slocum, a Squaxin Indian living on Mud Bay near Olympia, Washington, "died" at four o'clock in the morning. The family sent messengers to Olympia with a canoe to secure a casket. At two o'clock in the afternoon, John revived, and messengers were sent to cancel the order for the casket.

Slocum immediately told of the experiences of the time he had been "dead." He had gone to the gate of heaven but had been turned back because, the angels said, his heart was not clean. He was permitted to look back and see his body stretched out, being prepared for burial. He was also given a revelation that the Most High God had a Son named Jesus who had died for the Indians and that unless the Indians believed in Jesus and had their hearts cleansed, they could not come to heaven. Slocum was then allowed to return to his body, provided he would preach the message he had received.

Folks nod their heads, with tongue in cheek, at the

telling of this story and rationalize it by saying that Slocum was just in a coma, and, during the coma, this bit of information came back from his subconscious mind, something he had heard from missionaries at some time in the past. Slocum was about forty years old when this event happened.

Whatever the explanation, there are still some rather pertinent facts that have emerged from the investigation of the situation, that demand explanation. The Squaxin Indians were an obscure, poverty-ridden little tribe living along the sloughs of Skookum Creek, where it entered into Mud Bay, on an arm of Puget Sound. They had little or no contact with the areas where missionary work had been done and had never been visited by a missionary, as far as anyone knows. John Slocum had been baptized, as a baby, by a passing Catholic priest, but no one in the obscure little tribe had any knowledge of Christianity. The missionary to the Skokomish Indians, Myron Eels, and his brother, who was Indian agent for the area, paid no attention to the Squaxins. Slocum, whose Indian name was Squ Sacht Un, was totally illiterate and knew no English. The tribe, in 1890, numbered less than fifty members.

Whatever the circumstances or the means by which Slocum came to know the name of Jesus, it is a known fact that a transformation took place in his life and the lives of those who were influenced by his "vision." James Wickersham, describing him, said, "He was looked upon as a common Indian with an inclination to fire water and pony racing as well as a known fondness for Indian gambling." Wickersham further stated, "While he may once have been, as he says, a drunkard, he is now a Christian man."

One of the early Squaxin converts, Louis Youaluck, gave this testimony:

"We were about the poorest tribe on earth. We were the only tribe now full blood and nothing else. We would not believe anything. Minister come here, but we laugh at him. We loved bad habits—gambling—stealing. And then John Slocum died. He was not a religious man—knew nothing of God—all of us same. We heard there was a God from Slocum. We could see it. Same time we heard of God we believe it. I was worst of lot. I was drunk and half starving—spent every cent for whiskey. I gambled, raced horses, bet shirt, money, blankets. I did not know any better.

"John Slocum brought good news to us; his words civilized us. We could see. We all felt blind those times. John Slocum came alive, and I remembered God and felt frightened. Now I have quit swearing. My heart is upside down; it is changed. If you don't believe in Christ you will go into a big fire and burn forever. I will remain a follower of Christ as long as I live."

Slocum, Mud Bay Sam, and Louis Youaluck started out preaching every day and everywhere along the lower end of Puget Sound, and many accepted the message.

So irregular were the methods of these men that the missionary to the Skokomish Indians to the north of the Squaxins was considerably disturbed. Through his brother the Indian agent, he had Slocum and Mud Bay Sam thrown in jail at Puyallup, where they languished for six months without any specific charge laid to them.

Judge Wickersham came to their rescue, had them released, and saw to it that a bill was passed in the state legislature which allowed the "irregular" group to worship as they pleased. Another bill was enacted making it a felony to disturb any religious meeting in the state of Washington.

Roman Catholic elements tried to take the new church into its orbit, but again, by process of law, the group was given its autonomy. A few artifacts of the Catholic church clung to the movement, such as the cruciform, sacred pictures, candles, and bells. These are more evident in some church buildings than in others. The interesting fact is that present-day members apparently are not aware of the source of these things and have attached new meanings and utility to them.

Silas Heck, the only living Indian to remember the emergence of the new church, when I asked about these artifacts, said that there is no doubt but that Mud Bay Louis, who had been a Roman Catholic, brought these things into the church. He explained further that they really didn't mean much because "when Jesus comes, they will all be burned up like everything else that is man-made."

The movement has continued until the present. The Indian name is the Tschaddam church. This is probably a Squaxin word, but this cannot be confirmed as there are no remaining Squaxins who know the old language. The whites gave the name of "Shaker" to the group because of the enthusiasm with which they worshiped at times. Judge Wickersham, in a letter to anthropologist James Mooney, says: "In times of excitement many of them twitch and shake, but in no instance do they conduct themselves as I have seen orthodox white Christians do at Old Sandy Branch camp meeting in Illinois."*

The Shakers are the only group in the Pacific Northwest who have been consistently free from the white man's or the usual Indian's vices. Their doctrinal statement is meager and underwritten. They express their belief somewhat as follows: "We believe that the Most High God had a Son named Jesus, who died for the Indians and that unless we believe in Him and have our hearts cleaned, we cannot go to heaven. We believe that the Holy Spirit teaches us and leads us in our worship." The group ranges from the Hupa reservation in northern California to Vancouver Island, B. C., and east to the Yakima reservation in eastern Washington, and the Warm Springs reservation in Oregon.

*James Mooney, *The Ghost Dance Religion* (Washington, D.C.: Government Printing Office, 1896), pp. 751-54.

29

CHEHALIS

Silas Heck's board-and-batten cabin on the Chehalis Indian reservation is overgrown with vines and brambles, and the yard is filled with uncut weeds and grass. You would suppose that no one lived there, except that a calico cat is sitting on the step by an empty saucer, anticipating the next meal. A rap on the door elicits a hearty "Come."

It is pretty dark inside, because the windows are overgrown with the brambles; but that doesn't bother Mr. Heck. He is blind and ninety-two years old.

After the eyes become adjusted to the dim light, one sees a clutter of papers, cartons, and odd pieces of furniture with a pathway from the bed to the other end of the room which serves as a kitchen. An extension of the path leads to the back door.

One also sees a book case with a rather judicious selection of reference books and other matter. Dust has accumulated on the books, but the old man's mind—quite unimpaired by the flight of time—is well aware of the contents. His formal schooling was meager, but he is quite well informed and speaks with a better than average English and without any fuzziness of diction.

In addition to his knowledge of the world in general, he has an inexhaustible store of the unwritten lore and history of his Chehalis people and the other Salish tribes of the north Pacific Coast.

Anthropologists and linguists have visited many times in the little cabin through the years, because the old man's memory, coupled with what he learned from his grandmother who died at age one hundred and five, spans the years back to the late 1700s.

I always visit the old gentleman when in the Northwest, and he invariably fills me in on something I have never heard before. When I saw him about the time of his ninety-second birthday, he was quite pleased and seemed more talkative than usual. He said, "Those anthropologist fellows always make fun of my stories when they go away and write things that I don't really say; but you always read the Bible and pray with me, so I like to tell you stories about the old ones. Maybe you will write them down so that, when this old man is gone, the stories of the Chehalis people will not be lost."

On another visit he told me about how some of his people and some of the Yakimas knew about and worshiped the Most High God. They had a colloquial name for Him, but the concept was biblically true. The greater number of the tribes of the Northwest worshiped, or at least feared, the woodland spirits known as the Timanawas, who seemed to represent the accumulated power of the departed ancestors. The early missionaries that came to these tribes ignored the fact that at least some of these people had a knowledge of God, which they probably brought with them when they came to this continent.

The old man said, "You fellows, when you came, told us that we knew nothing of God and that we worshiped the devil, and that you were the only ones that knew about the true God."

A prayer of the old people, that was taught to Silas as a young man by his Yakima mother-in-law, is translated as follows:

O Thou Greatest Great and Highest High!
We thank You for all the good things You send from above.
We thank You for the forest, where the deer can hide;
We thank You for giving them to us for food.
We thank You for the streams, where the salmon swim;
We thank You for giving them to us for food.
We thank You for the birds, which give us songs.
We thank You for the sun to give us light and warmth.

O Thou Greatest Great and Highest High!
When You pass by this way, stop and pity us—
Not because we are worthy, for we are most unworthy;
Not because we are good, because our hearts are bad;
But because You made us and because we need You—
And lead us to Your life everlasting.

The old man then said in almost a whisper, "You fellows, when you came, didn't tell us that your Jesus was our "Greatest Great and Highest High."

Mr. Heck is the only living Indian who passed through the John Slocum excitement of the 1880s, and for some years he wandered throughout the Olympic Peninsula area as an evangelist of the Indian church among the Indian tribes. Apparently he was quite successful and quite aware of the vitality of the Christian message. He always walked, carrying a handball, such as was used by the bull cooks in the logging camps. This was his musical instrument. He carried candles for light. He slept wherever nightfall overtook him and ate what was given him or gathered berries and other items of food.

On one occasion he was overtaken on a rather lonely road by a traveling salesman and given a ride. The young man seemed quite despondent and was glad for any sort of human companionship. Mr. Heck told him that maybe he, like the Indians, could call on the Son of the Great Spirit for a new heart. They stopped the car, and the salesman and the Indian went into the woods and knelt by a log. Silas told the Lord that here was a poor white man that needed a new heart, and would the Indian's Saviour please help this white man and take away his fears and give him a new heart? He would indeed, and the salesman went on his way a new creature.

30

COWLITZ RIVER

My first meeting with Grandma Ike was in the spring of 1933. Her eyes were dim but not too dim to execute an intricate pattern in the watertight basket that she was weaving. Her teeth were gone long ago, but she was able to "gum" the strands of fibre that she was working into her basket. Her mind was clear as a bell, clear enough, in fact, to recall incidents and situations more than a century old.

The old lady was sitting in her favorite spot on the ground in front of her little cabin which was situated on a high bluff overlooking the delta of the Cowlitz and Tilton Rivers, on the fir-clad western slope of the Cascade Range in western Washington. It was midmorning of a bright spring day. Wisps of fog still hovered over the river. Young men of the tribe were netting Chinook and silver salmon below the riffles.

Mrs. Ike was a member of the upper Cowlitz band of the Chehalis tribe, and her husband had been chief. The tribe was never large and had diminished to a few families living in scattered spots along the upper Cowlitz.

The site of the old lady's cabin is now under the backwater of an artificial lake.

There wasn't much conversation during our first visit. Grandma had lived too many years to give much recognition to the new, white missionary. In fact she retreated almost entirely into the Chinook jargon (the trade language of the Indians and trappers in the fur-trading days) on this visit, although she accepted a trifling gift with the closest thing to a smile that an Indian can muster. On the second and third visits, she started to open up, and eventually she told her whole story. She spoke in a mixture of English and Chinook jargon with a typical economy of words, which makes the story all the more attractive.

"Long time 'go, look down that way [pointing west], see much smoke. Not Indian make smoke. Indian always make small smoke. My *kloochman* he say, 'We go see big smoke.' We take small baby, walk all day. Go to what white man call Cowlitz Prairie. Boston man* there, cut down much tree, make big fire, make big house with tree. My *kloochman* he see other kind Indian with white man. He ask Indian, 'What these white men do?' He say, 'These Hudson Bay men. Come to buy furs and dry salmon. Trade with Indian. You tell your people come bring furs to trade."

Checking back in our history, we find that the Hudson Bay Company did build a trading post on Cowlitz Prairie about 1832, as a way station between the Columbia River and Puget Sound. If Mrs. Ike was then

* A term used by the Indians of the Northwest for the early fur traders, many of whom came from Boston.

a mother with her first child, probably at the age of sixteen or seventeen, she would have been one hundred and sixteen when I first met her. The story continued:

"My people take furs and dry salmon to white-man trading post. White man give knives and cloth but mostly whiskey. Get Indians all drunk. They fight and yell and go crazy. Come back up river sick and furs all gone."

Inventory sheets of the old trading outfits of the Hudson Bay Company of that period show trifling amounts of legitimate trade goods and enormous quantities of rum, which was traded for furs in the proportion of one quart of watered-down rum for one marten skin. One episode of trading in this style over in British Columbia records that all of the tribe—men, women and children—were so drunk that they could not walk. The traders in this case traded with watered-down rum until not a pelt was left for trading. The Cowlitz band received the same treatment.

Mrs. Ike continued: "My people get more furs, go back to white-man trading post, get more whiskey. After while everybody drink all time. Then they get white-man diseases. Get sick in here [tapping her chest]. My sons die. My *kloochman* die. My people all sick. Pretty soon all gone."

The fur traders, in their ruthless competition for the furs of the Indians, had little place in their expeditions for real missionaries. The first fifty years of contact with the Rocky Mountain and Pacific Coast tribes saw no worthwhile missionary work accomplished, except in a few instances. The Spaldings and McBeth sisters did an amazing work among the Nez Perces in Idaho. Marcus Whitman and his party opened a mission among the Cayuses at Wailatpu, near to the present city of Walla Walla, Washington, but were massacred before their work bore any fruit. The Lees established a mission in the Willamette valley near the present city of Salem, Oregon, but soon abandoned it and went into trade.

Grandma Ike had known no white missionaries nor any white Christians until in her later years, when a few Christian families settled in the area at Harmony and Mossy Rock, and yet she had a basic Christian theology that was completely sound although utterly brief. I had asked the old lady if she knew Jesus Christ, probably a little timidly, because I had found that Indians generally have some suspicions when they think of Christianity as the white man's belief. They can't help associating the white man's religion with the other white man's traits that have caused such havoc among these primitive Americans. Mrs. Ike knew that there were white Christians, but she had come to know them after she, herself, had become a Christian, so there was no problem. The story of her conversion was as simple as her creed.

"My people get very bad—always drink, fight, gamble, race horses, get in jail. 'Bout forty years 'go, Chehalis Indian come from down river, go around families, ring hand bell, and tell everybody come one place. He tell how his friend, Indian name John Slocum, die one night and go to gate of heaven and get turn back because his heart bad. Angel at gate tell John Slocum he must go back and tell all Indians that High God in heaven have Son name Jesus, who die for Indians. All Indians must believe in Him and get clean heart or cannot come to heaven. John Slocum come alive in afternoon and tell story. He start preaching. Mud Bay Sam and Mud Bay Charlie believe and start preaching. These all bad man before. Now no more get drunk, fight, get in jail. My people listen. Some laugh and try to chase Chehalis Indian out. Some my people listen good and believe in Jesus. Quit bad things. My heart change inside."

A recent conversation with Silas Heck, one of the few remaining Indians who remember the John Slocum incident, confirmed the fact that a few of the upper Cowlitz band had been converted through the preaching and that the Ikes were among them. Mr. Heck's version was slightly different. He thought that one of their number, probably the chief himself, had come down river to a camp meeting, was converted, and took the message back with him.

My last visit with the old lady was a fitting climax to the five years of fellowship we had enjoyed. It was fall. She had just returned with her tribe from the higher mountains where they picked huckleberries each year and dried them. The place was about fifteen miles from her home, and it always took Grandma two days to make the trip. When night came, she would make a bed for herself in the brush and continue her trip the next day.

Her larder was complete for winter. There were huge slabs of dried salmon hanging on a wire, hard as a rock and as black as the old lady's skin; a good fat sack of dried huckleberries, and a sack of whole wheat. Quite a diet for a toothless woman one hundred and twenty years old, but it was all she wanted and all she needed, and she had plenty of time to "gum" the dry salmon and whole wheat. This was a good-bye visit, and I was dressing her bad foot for the last time.

She said, "I be long time here. My old friends all gone. Most my family gone. But pretty soon Papa Jesus come, take me home. No more tired body, no more sore feet."

31

INDIAN CRADLE BOARDS

The Indian cradle board is an intriguing and very practical device. Indian babies are quite contented in them and, when taken out, will cry to be put back in them.

They can be carried handily on the back or suspended from the horn of the saddle for traveling. Baby can be put out of harm's way by being hung on a peg on the wall or leaned against the wall.

It was a common sight, a few years back, to see a row of Paiute cradle boards, complete with round, dark faces, leaning against the side wall of the Arrowhead Hotel in Burns, Oregon, while the mothers were doing their trading around town. Of course, there was the inconvenience of having an occasional stray dog proceed along the row and lick the gummy little faces. But maybe there was satisfaction even in this to both the dog and the babies: the dog got some nourishment, and the babies had their faces washed.

"Yes, but how about—?"

Well, you see, Indian mothers invented the disposable diaper. In desert country, the women shred the inner bark of several shrubs and trees and make a soft, cozy, and absorbent nest for baby to lie in. Over on the Northwest coast they gathered the abundant quantities of moss from the maple trees for baby's nest.

Grandma Ike, who occupied the previous chapter, had the habit of dropping in for the day to visit her white neighbors. She would sit in one spot for hours, just watching. She didn't say much, but what little she did say was usually the concentrated expression of a great deal of observing and cogitation.

One day she visited a young neighbor housewife who currently had two in diapers. The old lady sat, without speaking, while the young mother washed and rinsed and hung up endless yardages of baby things on the clothesline.

Finally the last tubful was on the line, and the young mother slumped to a seat in exhaustion. Grandma Ike studied her for a while and then took another look at the endless line of white things fluttering in the breeze. She rose and started slowly away with the sage comment, "Moss is easier!"

32

MARY KIONE'S LAST BASKET

The old lady was puttering around with what seemed to be a jumble of worthless odds and ends. As the observer looked more closely, however, it could be seen that Mary Kione was actually creating a basket.

In her deft hands, this, her last basket, would be the crowning masterpiece of her lifetime of skilled craftsmanship. All of Mary's baskets were collectors' items and, now that she is gone, are priceless.

In the inventory of odds and ends were coils of sweet grass hanging to dry on the picket fence. There were bundles of creamy white spruce roots and strands of the inner bark of red cedar. An old shoe box was filled with the breast feathers of robins, the blue-gray wing feathers of the blue jay, the scarlet crests of woodpeckers, and the hackles from a pheasant's neck.

Out of this miscellany, Mary would not make a basket to sell. Who could buy the product of the accumulated skill of a century of creating by a consummate artist? She would give the basket to some young friend who would treasure it for its creator's sake.

Mary Kione was the last of the original stock of the Upper Cowlitz tribe. She lived and died in her little valley where the glacier-born Cowlitz River cascades down from the slopes of Mount Rainier.

Her birth year was about 1845. We dated this from the fact that, as a girl, she remembered vividly the commotion of the exploring party sent by Governor Isaac Ingalls Stevens to explore a route over the cascades for a transcontinental railroad. The Chinook Pass, below which Mary's tribe lived was explored but rejected as too formidable for a railroad grade. It would be another century before an automobile road would take this route.

The Upper Cowlitz tribe had been formed many generations ago from the elements of two tribes, the Chehalis and the Yakima. The Yakimas came up from their valley in the east each fall for hunting in the high pass. The Chehalis would come up from the west. A meeting of the tribes would occur each year, and young folks of each tribe would get together. A new tribe was formed which took up its dwelling in the meadows lower down the slope of the Cowlitz. Over the years as the tribes met and fraternized, a new jargon, composed of both languages, developed. Mary was the last to speak this language.

The tribe was now reduced to a handful. White man's diseases took their toll. Young people went out of the valley to marry in other tribes. The old ones had died—all except Mary. The crowding of the white man's culture was more restrained in these canyons than in most cases. The little band lived in a secluded tree-trimmed meadow of a hundred acres. Kione Creek ran through it. The white man's big road was a mile away, and the whine of the sawmill was modified to a muted hum by the music of the river. An unspoiled patch of woodland and undergrowth gave shelter to grouse and song birds.

Mary got out to "civilization" a few times in her life, enough to get her name and picture in the paper: "Lewis County claims the oldest living Indian in the state of Washington." But at age one hundred eighteen, Mary went back to her valley and the little Indian cemetery.

I asked Silas Heck, our old Chehalis friend, if he knew Mary.

"That old lady? Sure, I've known her all my life." Silas was ninety-three at the time.

Did the gospel message ever reach Mary's valley?

The years, eighty-five of them, rolled back in the old man's mind. "I remember," he said, "it was the time that John Slocum had his vision about the beautiful country where God lived. John Slocum and Mud Bay Sam and Louis Howaluck were preaching about the vision and telling all the folks that if they believed in Jesus and had their hearts cleansed, they could come to His beautiful place above.

"Indians from all over heard of the vision and came to Mud Bay to see what had happened. They believed and had their hearts cleansed and then went out over the trails, up and down the coast and over the mountains. John Ike came from the upper country and went back with the message. Mary and her tribe heard the Gospel from him."

That was in 1882. John and his wife (Grandma Ike)

built a little church on the banks of the Cowlitz at Harmony, some forty miles from Mary's valley. She and her tribe used to walk down to Harmony for meetings which would extend for several days at a time.

The little chapel is gone. Its site is under the waters of Mayfield Lake, and a beautiful area of woodland and lake shore is named "Mary Kione Park."

Tourists from San Jose and Walla Walla park their campers, cast for rainbow trout, and say, "I wonder who Mary Kione was."